The Resilience and Wellbeing Toolbox is an
for educators looking for hands-on ideas to
emotional wellbeing. Based in sound research, this book is much more than a
collection of activities – it incorporates knowledge on how children develop
and learn, what they need to flourish and ways to build both individual and
community wellbeing. The book's flexible format enables it to be used with
individuals, groups or whole classes. Many activities are ideal for use in Circle
work. The innovative Tips for Parents to reinforce learning at home are especially
welcome.

—**Dr Sue Roffey**, FRSA, Associate Professor (adjunct),
School of Education, Western Sydney University, Australia

Madhavi Nawana Parker has worked extensively with Pembroke School staff
and parents to help us better understand and support behaviour, resilience and
social-emotional learning. Her presentations and workshops have been
engaging, entertaining and downright common sense for often overwhelmed
parents and educators. She has also helped us to demystify some challenging
behaviours. *The Resilience and Wellbeing Toolbox* is a wonderful assemblage
of Madhavi's ideas, strategies and learnings from many years of nourishing
families and young people and their schools. Schools often lament the lack of
resilience in their students but struggle to implement opportunities to build this.
Here are some answers.

—**Jamie Holland**, Dean of Student Welfare,
Pembroke School, South Australia

The Resilience and Wellbeing Toolbox is a fantastic resource which challenges
us as parents/carers to think about how we can further support our children.
It offers helpful strategies and worksheets on problem solving, compromise,
stress management, goal setting and more.

—**Leanne Kutschbach**, parent

The Resilience and Wellbeing Toolbox

The Resilience and Wellbeing Toolbox is an inspiring book and a beacon for social emotional change in schools. Within these pages teachers and other professionals will find fantastic resources that they can easily implement in the classroom. By following this programme, teachers will see their students developing skills in persistence, problem solving and emotional regulation as well as independence, empathy, kindness, contribution and good will, whilst planting the essential seeds of resilience and wellbeing. Helpful suggestions offered in each chapter on how to bring wellbeing and resilience into the home can be shared with parents and families.

The lively and engaging resources in this book include:

- Practical, photocopiable guide sheets and worksheets
- Adaptable role plays and activities
- Solid research-based strategies
- A flexible framework that can be creatively implemented in the classroom.

This is a must-have handbook for anyone seeking to provide young people in their care with a strong foundation for better social, emotional and learning outcomes.

Madhavi Nawana Parker is a behaviour consultant in private practice, based in Australia. She has previously published with Routledge *What's the Buzz?* (2011) and *What's the Buzz? for Early Learners* (2015) with Mark Le Messurier.

The Resilience and Wellbeing Toolbox

A guide for educators and health professionals

Madhavi Nawana Parker

Routledge
Taylor & Francis Group

LONDON AND NEW YORK

First published 2017
by Routledge
2 Park Square, Milton Park, Abingdon, Oxon OX14 4RN

and by Routledge
711 Third Avenue, New York, NY 10017

Routledge is an imprint of the Taylor & Francis Group, an informa business

British Library Cataloguing in Publication Data
A catalogue record for this book is available from the British Library

Library of Congress Cataloging in Publication Data
Names: Parker, Madhavi Nawana, author.
Title: The resilience and wellbeing toolbox: a guide for educators and health professionals / Madhavi Nawana Parker.
Description: New York, NY : Routledge, 2017.
Identifiers: LCCN 2016020635 | ISBN 9781138921153 (hardback) | ISBN 9781138921177 (pbk.) | ISBN 9781315679365 (ebook)
Subjects: LCSH: Affective education. | Gratitude.
Classification: LCC LB1072. P37 2017 | DDC 370.15/34—dc23
LC record available at https://lccn.loc.gov/2016020635

ISBN: 978-1-138-92115-3 (hbk)
ISBN: 978-1-138-92117-7 (pbk)
ISBN: 978-1-315-67936-5 (ebk)

Typeset in Helvetica
by Keystroke, Neville Lodge, Tettenhall, Wolverhampton

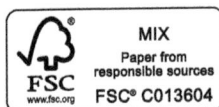

MIX
Paper from
responsible sources
FSC
www.fsc.org   FSC® C013604

Printed and bound by CPI Group (UK) Ltd, Croydon, CR0 4YY

The Resilience and Wellbeing Toolbox is dedicated to our children, Soraya, Toby and Zach Nawana Parker, with love always, Mum

Contents

Acknowledgements   xi

Introduction   1
Brainstorms 14
Journal entry 15
My 5 point self-rating scale 16

1   Gratitude, perspective and optimism   18
    From the low side (unhelpful thinking) to the high side
       (helpful thinking) 37
    Active mood combat 38
    7 day gratitude record sheet 39

2   Knowing your values and sticking to them   41
    Finding my values 58
    Values guide sheet 59
    Who am I? 60
    Me and my favourite things 61
    Values for my resilience and wellbeing 62
    If it was up to me 63
    Things bigger than me survey 64

3   Community and connection: the importance of empathy and
    belonging in relationships   66
    Empathy: how will you take action? 91
    Connect-a-thon: watch me connect with others 92
    Teacher report 93
    Kindness record sheet 94

4   Problem solving   96
    Be the boss of problem solving 113
    Problem solving: working out the pluses and minuses 114
    Solving problems with friends: guide sheet 115
    Writing a riddle: guide sheet 116

x Contents

5 Keeping calm 118
My body when it's not calm 142
'I can handle it': calming ideas 143
My stress less plan 144
How big does this rate? From ants to dinosaurs 145
Going with the 'flow' survey 146
6 tricks to keep calm 147
What makes me angry? 148
What I do when I am angry 149

6 Embracing mistakes through curiosity 151
Best mistake ever 166
*Questions to ask young people to encourage self-awareness
    and help students learn from mistakes 167*

7 Persistence and the value of hard work 169
Mountains of persistence 186
Persistence challenge 187
Motivation survey 188
Effort self-assessment 189

8 Setting goals 191
7 steps to my goal: worksheet 207
7 steps to my goal: worksheet 208
7 steps to my goal: example 209
'Can I? – Can't I?' 210

Recommended reading for young people 212
Index 214

Acknowledgements

Professional thanks and acknowledgements

This book would not have been possible without the following people. I thank you all for your kind and generous support:

Amanda Harris, my first professional mentor. Thank you for the clap-worthy dinners and for your balanced, playful perspective. Nicolle Stephanos for finding my keys and coming for the ride. Always generous with your time, energy, and friendship. Mark Le Messurier for our first-born, *What's the Buzz?* and all the wonderful adventures that followed. Rose Price for your friendship and our annual trips to Pt Moorowie where much inspiration for this book was drawn sitting on your deck. Autism SA where my passion and drive for this work began. Fullarton House, Scotch College and Pulteney Grammar School for being such brilliant workplaces to belong to. Schools around Adelaide who enthusiastically trialled the manuscript and gave feedback along the way. Sue Roffey, Virginia Evans and Jaimie Holland, all sources of inspiration for young people, thank you for reviewing my manuscript, despite your very full work agendas. All the families and students that keep me focused on my professional goals and are a joy and inspiration to work with. Lauren Eldridge-Murray for all the late nights spent illustrating this book with such dedication, creativity and enthusiasm. James Parker for editing and helping guide this book. Lucy Lokan for preparing the manuscript for publishing. Alison Foyle at Routledge, for your confidence in this book from the beginning and for your encouragement and dedication throughout the process. Sarah Tuckwell and the production team at Routledge, for being such a pleasure to work with. The wonderful team at Keystroke for their incredible team work and care. Thank you also to the young people featured in this book for their inspiring stories of resilience and wellbeing: Birke Baehr, Mackenzie Bearup, Brittany Bergquist, Thandiwe Chama, Maren Johnson, Lennon Maher, Efren Peñaflorida Jr. and Evans Wading.

Personal thanks

To my parents Srinath Nawana (1939–1984) and Mallika Nawana for whom I am grateful every day. Thank you for giving me a lifelong love of learning and for your guidance and confidence along the way. You showed courage and love throughout your lives and led the way for your three children; teaching me, how to lead the way for ours. My husband, James, for your never-ending love, wisdom, hard work, humour and dedication to me and our children. Our children, Soraya, Toby and Zach, the light of my life. Thank you for your abundant laughter, love and enthusiasm. You make every day the best day. My treasured nieces and nephews, Dylan, Eléa, Tylanni and Naél, who bring me so much joy with their curiosity, creativity and love. My very special monkey hugger for sharing your birthday and for your loyalty, honesty, guidance, humour and encouragement throughout my life. Erica, my mother-in-law, for bringing James into the world and for being a special friend to me and our children. My friends, old and new, for all the laughter, support and learning we share. I am grateful to all of you. A special thanks (in order of appearance) to Sally Bolton (talking and listening since '86), Tania Campbell, Ange O'Halloran, Leanne Schmidt, Rebecca Barr, Amanda Harris, Melanie Dolphin, Nicolle Bowering, Kate Rayner, the MP-PMMG (Katie O'Reilly, Audrey Woodrow and Vashti Forbes), Vanessa Wigg and Sascha Smith. Thank you all for being a source of joy, love and inspiration throughout so many stages of my life.

Introduction

Welcome to *The Resilience and Wellbeing Toolbox*. Perhaps you picked up this guide intrigued by the growing emphasis in education and health about the value of developing resilience and improving wellbeing. Or maybe the topic is new to you and focusing on better mental health naturally fits in with your values.

Either way, as a teacher, educator, health professional or parent, the resilience and wellbeing of young people will often feel very much your responsibility. As important as teaching the foundation skills underlying these two strengths is, the resilience and wellbeing of young people springs largely from strong healthy connections in the young person's life (Werner and Smith, 2001). Your genuine care and commitment itself is already making a difference.

Before going any further, I wish to emphasise that although *The Resilience and Wellbeing Toolbox* is full of many useful strategies, ideas and activities, enhanced resilience and wellbeing is the by-product of many things working together. They cannot be taught as isolated skills like you can teach someone to read or to ride a bike. There are so many factors involved in developing resilience and wellbeing and this book offers a starting point rather than providing a complete curriculum.

The development of resilience is a process; a combined result of many things that happen across the lifetime, the skills developed along the way and an influence of individual personalities and temperaments (Hall and Pearson, 2007). It must be recognised that each child is unique and develops in their own way and in their own time. Resilience and wellbeing cannot be forced. Pushing to build and nurture resilience in young people can be counter-productive. Trying too hard to teach these skills and placing pressure on young people to do so can reduce wellbeing. Young people know when the adults most important to them are under pressure and inevitably absorb their second-hand stress. Feeling compelled to commit a significant amount of time teaching these skills in addition to all the other things you're responsible for could easily lead to resilience and wellbeing fatigue – for you!

This book allows you to take things as quickly or slowly as you wish and to be as creative as you like in implementation of its ideas. It respects that much of the expertise lies firmly within the young person's support network and when skills are taught through strong and caring relationships, young people inevitably thrive. Keeping this in mind, remember the suggestions in this book are not prescriptive and the guide sheets, worksheets, discussions, role plays and activities can be used in many different ways to match your time, energy and classroom climate. You can easily spend a month or more focusing on one chapter, grabbing five-minute bursts of discussion, worksheets or activities where you can, while adding your own knowledge on the topic into the mix. Or, you can dedicate a focused 45-minute to one-hour session each week, which will generally allow you three sessions to cover all the activities in each chapter. You are the best judge of how to implement the ideas offered within these pages. Let your instinct and experience guide you.

The Resilience and Wellbeing Toolbox is based on decades of solid research without attempting to cover all aspects of wellbeing and resilience. It offers you a flexible framework to teach students self-discipline and self-awareness, emotional regulation, persistence, problem solving, goal setting, values, empathy and gratitude. Each chapter offers ways to build young people's knowledge and abilities in each area. It is by no means exhaustive; it is a beginning.

How to use this book

This book is not prescriptive. It can be used with individuals, small groups and classes. In an education setting it can be used as a whole school approach to wellbeing and resilience, complementing other social emotional learning programs already existing in schools. When used as a whole school approach, students can consolidate skills more easily when the broader school community is using the same language and ideas. Families also benefit when siblings at the same school bring home discussions they have learnt in their classes, further embedding the benefits of this program in the broader community.

Health professionals can use this program to build skills in young people through sessions with individuals or together in small groups. Many of the activities refer to classroom groups and small group activities within the context of the classroom; however in a health care setting, these activities can be implemented and adapted where necessary with one child or in a group with a supporting health professional.

Activities are easy to use and require little, if any, planning. Materials are minimal and where necessary are easily sourced. Most activities can be enjoyed as much by early learning and junior primary students as they are by students in upper primary. Early learning and junior primary students will sometimes need help developing their understanding but the program is easily adaptable. Secondary schools can also use the program to build students' awareness and understanding about resilience and wellbeing by reflecting on the tales about other young people with resilience, developing deeper understanding through the explanations, engaging in the discussions, brainstorming and journaling. There are also many hands-on activities that secondary students will enjoy the opportunity to play about with.

Program values

An outline is provided below showing the program values. Posting these up and reminding students about them is a great way to reinforce the program goals. When students present with challenging behaviour, you can gently refer them back to the program values. You can also use the program values as a motivational framework for rewards as individuals or as a group. For example, students work towards upholding the program values and are rewarded for their efforts and outcomes in these areas. It can also be helpful to provide parents with a copy of the values for consistency. Some families use these values in their home to complement the program.

The Resilience and Wellbeing Toolbox values

Work hard
Keep calm
Have courage
Give thanks
Care about others
Learn from mistakes

Session structure

Each chapter focuses on a new resilience and wellbeing skill, broken down into various steps and stages. Core sections are not grouped together sequentially as developing the individual aspects of each skill often needs a multi-stage approach. This might mean some 'understanding' time, some 'how to' time, a handful of 'role plays' and some 'practice' time for each component of the overall skill. The core chapter sections are as follows:

1   Introduction. This section is largely for the facilitator and parents to read to develop a context for teaching the skill and an understanding about why the skill is valuable for resilience and wellbeing. It is recognised with a

2   An explanation (for younger and older students). This section is written for the program facilitator to explain the skill to their students. It can be read to the students or reworded as suitable. This section is recognised with a

3   A short story about a young person who is recognised for using a specific skill. This section is recognised with a

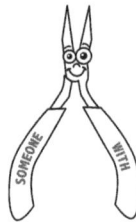

4   'Let's talk' is where group discussions and brainstorms encourage students to explore their thoughts and ideas openly and non-judgementally. The section is recognised with a

5   'How to' is the section showing how the skill is broken down into smaller steps for students to develop the skill. It often has guide sheets, worksheets and visual information about how to build a skill. This section is identified with a

6   'Role play' is the section where students can test out their skills and understanding by practising them in a role play. Role plays provide young people with an opportunity to explore many different ways in which one skill can be used and how to problem solve through situations that require the skill to be implemented. Facilitators can add their own role plays to the ones already offered in each chapter to make them more relevant to their cohort of students, as well as to encourage deeper understanding. This section is identified with a

7   'Practice' is the section full of games and activities to use the skill and practise it. It is identified with a

8   Weekly challenges are offered as an opportunity for students to set a goal to practise the skill outside of school to make changes in their lives.

9   Parent tips. Each chapter ends with a handful of parent tips (which many education and health professionals find useful in their teaching and therapeutic work as well), to encourage skill generalisation to home. It is identified with a

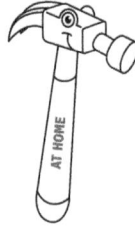

How long should be spent teaching each skill?

Each chapter contains approximately two to three hours of activity time in total. Sessions tend to work well in 45-minute to one-hour blocks. Each chapter can usually be covered in two to four sessions, depending on the group and facilitation style. When a session time cannot be allocated, the 'Resilience and Wellbeing Toolbox' can also be offered in short bursts, one activity at a time, over a longer period of time.

The Resilience and Wellbeing Toolbox can be run in a variety of ways with individuals or groups:

1   Sequentially, chapter by chapter, over numerous sessions. The facilitator completes as much of the chapter as possible, in order, over the allocated session time. The session ends with a sense of 'to be continued'.

2   Choosing one activity from each core section for the allocated time, giving students a broader overview. For example, you might talk about the skill, then take on a worksheet, do one lot of role plays and one activity before finishing. You would then follow a similar pattern for one or two more sessions until all the activities are completed.

3   As a group focus over several weeks using short five- to ten-minute bursts where time permits or whenever the group could do with a change of pace. To make this effective you would keep the chapter skill as a theme for the period you focused on it and do at least three five-minute activities a week.

What if an activity is too easy or too challenging for a group of students?

Chronological age is not always a good indication of abilities and interests. While this program offers activities for students as young as kindergarten age and as old as secondary school, use your judgement to adjust the pace and content where an activity needs tweaking. Where possible, younger students are offered alternative activities, visual instruction and more simplified explanations. Younger students will also benefit from the use of a whiteboard or projector and puppets to help them understand the skills at a deeper level. Older students may only need information about the skill, guide sheets, role plays and a handful of activities to understand the skill and further develop it. For students in upper primary or secondary school you might only spend one session per chapter.

Students with learning or developmental difficulties will benefit from the program being adjusted to match their personal learning abilities and interests.

THIS PROGRAM DOES NOT AIM TO 'FIX' FEELINGS, CHARACTER OR BEHAVIOUR: THIS PROGRAM TEACHES SKILLS TO REGULATE FEELINGS, BUILD CHARACTER AND DEVELOP VALUES TO HELP YOUNG PEOPLE MAKE BETTER CHOICES FOR BETTER BEHAVIOUR.

Young people develop in their own time. Personality, temperament, genetics and environment can all play a part. It is important for children to hear the message that they are accepted for who they are, even when they struggle with their moods, values and behaviour. When children sense that someone is trying to 'fix' them and does not accept them for who they are, relationships can suffer. This does not mean you do not keep boundaries or limits on behaviour, but rather the feedback you give separates the behaviour from the person.

Living in a 'fix it' culture where children are sometimes over-protected or rescued from challenging life experiences can also mean resilience and wellbeing are lowered. Shielding young people from sadness, discomfort, boredom and conflict in order to 'feel good' and 'happy' most of the time is not realistic or useful. The unintended side effect of this may sometimes be a young person who cannot cope when things go wrong, relying too heavily on those around them to make things better.

The Resilience and Wellbeing Toolbox encourages students to understand that life has ups and downs and a shift in mood will often quite naturally follow these events. Moods and feelings do not need to be 'fixed'. They need a combination of understanding and acceptance, problem solving, self-awareness and self-regulation. In each chapter, students will learn various skills that encourage better emotional regulation and coping skills that underlie higher resilience and wellbeing.

Neuroplasticity

Students can understand the value of new skills through repetition when introduced to the concept of neuroplasticity: the brain's ability to learn through repeated practice. Students as young as 4 can learn that their brain sends out signals between neurons each time they practise something new, and the more they use the skill the stronger the neural pathway becomes. Having knowledge like this can be very motivating for young people.

Encouragement in place of praise

The self-esteem movement at various stages tried to make all children feel special in the hope they would like themselves more, have better confidence and as a result perform better. Attempts were made to protect children from the disappointments that came from being anything other than first and best. Medals and certificates began to be awarded equally and praise was lavishly offered whether it was earned or not. You were special because you had brown hair (or black hair, or blonde or grey hair for that matter), you were special because you were an only child, and you were special because you were not an only child! Parents and teachers were taught to praise their children and students for every achievement. It did not matter whether or not the achievement was a result of hard work, good fortune or natural talent. These factors were irrelevant and children were praised to the tune of 'you're the best . . . you're so smart . . . you're brilliant at mathematics . . . you're a little artist . . .'; and their work was equally praised with 'this is beautiful . . . this is brilliant . . . perfect' and so on. Parents and teachers worked overtime making sure the self-esteem of all children was raised higher than Mount Everest!

The difficulty with such praise was that, after hearing the same thing over and over, children stopped believing what they were being told. This level of feedback focusing directly on labelling children as 'smart . . . artistic . . . beautiful', loses authenticity and value over time. It isn't related to the person underneath, or the behaviour that led to the achievement (persistence, time, luck, talent, self-belief and so forth), and it fails to highlight the effort involved in achievement. A focus on effort and the other variables associated with achievement is now associated with what develops self-esteem and enhances achievement (Dweck, 2012).

To make things worse, students lose the opportunity to self-reflect about their abilities and progress when they become reliant on what other people think of their abilities and progress. They become 'praise addicts', desperately seeking feedback from parents and teachers for reassurance they are doing okay. Self-esteem does not increase because someone else tells us how wonderful we are. Self-esteem increases when we own our efforts and understand their relationship to the outcomes of everything we do. It is also impacted strongly by our connection to something bigger than ourselves and a strong sense of integrity (Crocker, 2003).

A sense of self and achievement builds when students are a dynamic part of goal setting, skill building, character building, service, self-awareness and self-assessment. *The Resilience and Wellbeing Toolbox* provides many opportunities for students to develop in these areas without the need for external praise and approval.

Self-assessment and self-reflection

Encouraging students to reflect on their learning experience is an integral part of this program. Student self-assessment, whereby students self-monitor, self-evaluate, and identify better ways they can learn, has been found to be a critical skill enhancing student motivation and achievement (McMillan and Hearn, 2008; Hattie, 2008).

Rather than praising students for their work and telling them what you like about their work, students can be encouraged to ask themselves how they are performing, what they think of their work and how they feel they could improve. The addition of self-assessment helps students take responsibility for their own learning. They will also become more aware about their strengths, and gain a better idea of what they find interesting and challenging. Using this approach can be useful in all learning areas.

Questions to ask during key learning periods in the program to promote self-assessment and reflection

Self-judgement questions:
How are you going with this challenge?
How do you think you went with the test?
What do you think of your work?
Do you like what you have done?
What do you like about it?
What don't you like about it? (If anything.)
Did you find it challenging?
Did you find it easy?

Self-improvement questions:
Could you have done anything differently?
What could you have done more/less of to find this easier/more interesting?
What could have made it easier/more interesting?
What could I have done as your teacher/mentor to help you more with this task?

Self-monitoring questions:
Did you enjoy it?
Did you give it your best effort?
Do you think you stayed with the challenge even when it was tough?
What helped you persist?
What got in the way of persisting?
What part did you enjoy?
What part didn't you enjoy?
Were you surprised at how things turned out?
Would you like to try something like this again?

Journals

Providing students with a journal (a writing book is ample) to record their goals and experiences during their wellbeing and resilience development is a great way for you (and them) to keep track of their learning. The journal can be used to take notes during lessons, to paste photographs or drawings about lesson experiences and to record the weekly challenges. The weekly challenge formula for the journal is as follows:

Weekly challenge entry

My challenge this week is:

Three steps I can take towards reaching my challenge:
1
2
3
At the end of the week: more practice needed? (YES/NO)

Check-in time: set a time each day (an hour or so) where you ask students to be aware of their use of the skill you are currently focusing on. This allows students to remain focused on what they have learnt. Also remind your students you will have a 'secret' time each day where you are assessing their skills in the area just to keep them on their toes!

Learning through repetition and reminders

Most children need reminders when they are working to build a new skill. Set your students up for success by providing clear reminders about their goals throughout the program. This can be a poster, a note on the wall, a comment on the whiteboard, or a 'secret signal' (a thumbs up, a wink, a nod). Without reminders many students who have the best of intentions to build new skills simply forget to practise and work on them.

Weekly themes based on the program goal at the time are another great way to keep your students focused on what they are learning. It can also help create a cohesive outlook amongst the group. For example, if the class follows the theme of persistence, with a visual prompt on a pin-up board, whenever met with a challenge they are reminded to persist. Other students are also more likely to tune into someone who is struggling with the goal and offer some much needed moral support.

Celebration

If you are recording the effort your students are putting in to develop new skills, a small celebration every now and then is a great way to acknowledge effort and enjoy a chance to sit back and reflect. Celebrations can be a cooking activity, afternoon lessons taken outdoors, a neighbourhood discovery walk, or a cake! If you are looking for inspiration on how you might celebrate as a group – ask your students. They will have plenty of ideas!

Relationships

Your students learn well from people they like and feel liked by. An understanding teacher–student relationship and strong connections between peers are key factors in the overall classroom climate, behaviour and level of effort and engagement (Rimm-Kaufman, 2011). Most people thrive when connected to and understood by others. The less conflict in a relationship, the better the connection and opportunity for growth. Not all students will be easy to connect with, and some are often the centre of conflict and can make it difficult for peers to get along with each other. Maintaining open discussions that encourage empathy, respect, problem solving and forgiveness helps develop these relationships through both happy and challenging times.

Measuring a baseline and outcomes

At the beginning of using this program you may wish to use the 'Strengths and Difficulties Questionnaire' developed by UK child psychiatrist Robert N. Goodman. The questionnaire is a self-report inventory behavioural screening questionnaire suitable for assessing young people aged 2 to 17. It is straightforward to use and is readily available online. Parents, teachers and health professionals can use the questionnaire to gain information about where a student's skill level and emotional status is at the onset of any behavioural intervention and then take the questionnaire again at the end of the intervention to identify gains and areas still needing support. Young people over the age of 11 are able to take a self-assessment survey as well.

What next?

Once you have worked through this book you may wonder, where to from here? It is probably sensible and fair to yourself to take a break. You probably need it – education and health professionals who are the custodians of young people's health and wellbeing often do!

When you're ready for another challenge there are plenty of Social Emotional Learning (SEL) programs available, both through the public education government curriculum and through other books and resources. In the context of schools, research is clear that teaching social and emotional skills lays a strong foundation for better behavioural and academic outcomes (Weissberg et al., 2011). Programs that aim to teach the language of social interaction in simple ways can usually do nothing but good. In Australia, the www.kidsmatter.com website has a comprehensive list of SEL programs; www.whatsthebuzz.net.au offers information about the 'What's the Buzz?' social and emotional skills programs as well as links to other well-regarded programs for young people (Le Messurier and Nawana Parker, 2011, 2015).

Whatever program you choose next it will be worthwhile if it offers young people skills to know themselves, manage themselves and get along with others. It helps if the program is fun too! Remember there is rarely one solution to any given challenge and using a variety of social emotional learning programs over time provides a number of ways to tackle the everyday challenges for young people. Enjoy the ride!

BRAINSTORMS

Record your ideas and the ideas you hear in your group during a brainstorm here...

_____

_____

_____

_____

_____

_____

_____

_____

_____

_____

_____

_____

_____

_____

_____

_____

_____

_____

_____

_____

_____

_____

_____

_____

_____

_____

_____

_____

_____

_____

_____

_____

_____

JOURNAL ENTRY

My journal entry drawing

MY 5 POINT SELF-RATING SCALE

Listening to others about how much hard work and effort they notice you put in can help you stay focused on your goals. Rating yourself on your hard work and effort is another important way to stay focused.

Draw (or write about) what you are working on in the box. Rate yourself at the end of each day on how much effort and hard work you put in. Hard work and effort means a strong and proud brain!

What I Am Working On

5 POINT SELF-RATING SCALE

1. (not working hard enough yet)

2. (working on this a little bit)

3. (working hard half the time)

4. (working hard most of the time)

5. (working hard every day and feeling proud)

Day 1	Day 2	Day 3	Day 4	Day 5	Day 6	Day 7
1. 2. 3. 4. 5.	1. 2. 3. 4. 5.	1. 2. 3. 4. 5.	1. 2. 3. 4. 5.	1. 2. 3. 4. 5.	1. 2. 3. 4. 5.	1. 2. 3. 4. 5.

Reference list

Crocker, J. 2003. 'Level of Self Esteem and Contingencies of Self Worth: Unique Effects on Academic, Social, and Financial Problems in College Students'. *Personality and Social Pyschology Bulletin* Vol. 29 No. 701.

Dweck, C. 2012. *Mindset: How You Can Fulfil Your Potential*. London: Constable.

Hall, D. and Pearson, J. 2007. 'Critical Abilities Related to the Development of Resilience'. *Interaction* (Canadian Childcare Federation, Ottawa).

Hattie, J. 2008. *Visible Learning for Teachers: Maximizing Impact on Learning*. London: Routledge.

Le Messurier, M. 2009. *Teaching Tough Kids: Simple and Proven Strategies for Student Success*. London: Routledge.

Le Messurier, M. and Nawana Parker, M. 2011. *What's the Buzz: A Social Skills Enrichment Program for Primary Age Students*. London: Routledge.

Le Messurier, M and Nawana Parker, M. 2015. *What's the Buzz for Early Learners: A Complete Foundation Course*. London: Routledge.

McMillan, J. H. and Hearn, J. 2008. 'Student Self-Assessment: The Key to Stronger Student Motivation and Higher Achievement'. *Educational Horizons* Vol 87 No. 1, pp. 40–49.

Rimm-Kaufman, S. 2011. *Improving Students' Relationships with Teachers to Provide Essential Supports for Learning*. Washington, DC: American Psychological Association.

Weissberg, R. P. et al. 2011. 'The Impact of Enhancing Students' Social and Emotional Learning: A Meta-Analysis of School Based Universal Interventions'. *Child Development* Vol. 82 No. 1, pp. 405–432, 440.

Werner, E. and Smith, S. 2001. *Journeys from Childhood to Midlife: Risk Resilience and Recovery*. Ithaca, NY: Cornell University Press.

1 Gratitude, perspective and optimism

Do not spoil what you have by desiring what you have not; remember that what you now have was once among the things you only hoped for.

Epicurus

Introduction for teachers and health professionals

Being grateful for what you have, keeping things in perspective and looking on the bright side, seem easier said than done. When you're experiencing stress or new challenges, thoughts and feelings have a tendency to run away from you. Feeling gratitude, keeping things in perspective and remaining optimistic can be harder to do during difficult times.

The good news is, when a person is able to continue a gratitude practice despite any challenges they are experiencing, their wellbeing and resilience rise. Gratitude helps them focus on the warmth of positive relationships, the beauty of nature, luck, good will and everything else around them that *is* going well. When gratitude focuses on three things that went well each for a period of 21 days, wellbeing, empathy and happiness increase. Anxiety and stress reduce too (Emmons and McCullough, 2003; Seligman, 2011). Focusing on what you are thankful for also allows you to experience positive situations again in reflection, almost as if you were experiencing them all over again (Rubin, 2011).

Different perspectives: optimists and pessimists

Seligman (2007) suggests the difference between optimists and pessimists is about how setbacks and victories are interpreted. Optimists see setbacks as temporary, changeable and related to the present circumstances. Pessimists see setbacks as permanent, fixed, and globalise the setback to all aspects of their lives. Victories are viewed by optimists as long-term and seen as a reflection of how well their lives are going. Pessimists see victories as temporary, occurring because of luck and something unlikely to be repeated (Seligman, 2007).

Normalising challenges and setbacks is a good beginning point for helping young people develop a more realistic view of life and learning. Teaching young people that a variety of factors steer the course of your plans from one day to the next helps them develop perspective about why things don't always go according to plan. Relationships, friendships, health, work, sport, play and school deeply interconnect our lives and experiences with the lives and experiences of everyone around us. It would not be possible for things to go smoothly all the time with so much at play.

Add natural temperament, personality and environmental differences, and some people just find it easier to feel grateful and look on the bright side than others. Developing skills in gratitude, perspective and optimism in those who have a less sunny temperament is a process enhanced with time and practice. With practice, the brain's neuroplasticity allows stronger connections to develop in the areas of gratitude, good perspective and optimism, weakening old connections for negative perspective and pessimism.

This chapter looks at ways to develop a regular practice in gratitude, keep things in perspective and focus the mind on positive experiences.

Explanation for all students

Gratitude is about noticing and being thankful for what is going well and what you *do* have. People have a natural tendency to focus on what is wrong and what they *don't* have. Paying too much attention to what is not going well even has a name! It's called the 'Negative Bias' (Rozin et al., 2001; Baumeister et al., 2001).

In one study, researchers showed their subjects happy and positive photos along with some unhappy negative photos. Their brain's electrical activity was recorded the whole time and it could be seen that it reacted much more to negative images and for longer than it did for positive ones (Cacioppo et al., 2007).

By spending focused time every day noticing what is going well you can create pathways in your brain to notice what is going right! Gratitude can also help keep things in perspective and see that tough times don't last forever.

Optimism is a way of looking at your life by focusing on what is going well. Optimists also see any challenges as a chance to learn something new and they practise looking for solutions instead of staying stuck in the problem. Optimism in this chapter will be called 'helpful thinking' and 'the high side'. Pessimism in this chapter will be called 'unhelpful thinking' and 'the low side'.

Additional information for older students

You might have heard the sayings, 'look on the bright side' and 'every cloud has a silver lining'. People often say this kind of thing when someone is upset. What they're asking you to do is to be grateful for what you do have and to be optimistic that things will work out. Pessimists (the opposite of optimists) notice what is going wrong and are quick to find fault in others or blame others for what is not working out for them.

Someone with gratitude:

Maren Johnson: Global Soap Project's Youth Ambassador

When Maren Johnson was just 15 and heard that over 4 million people die each year from intestinal diseases caused by not having clean water and hygiene products like soap and clean water, she felt so much **gratitude** for what she had and decided to do something about those who did not have the same luxuries. She discovered the Global Soap Project, partnered with it and since then has collected thousands of pounds of recycled soap through her work. She has over 200 volunteers working under her personal guidance as their Youth Ambassador. She remained **optimistic** when many hotels were unsure about how they could save soap bars effectively, so she worked hard to educate them about helpful ways to do this. She explained the plight of families all over the world so the hotel owners were able to keep in **perspective** what their extra effort would mean for these families. Over 1,000 hotels across North America now work closely with the Global Soap Project, recycling around 30,000 bars of soap every week – bars of soap that would otherwise have been thrown out after only one or two uses. Maren has been included in Youth Service America's list of the 25 Most Powerful and Influential Young People in the World.

BRAINSTORM: The negative bias

What might make a negative bias even worse for some people?

Can you think of a time when your negative bias meant you missed out on doing something you might have really enjoyed?

Can you think of a time you ignored your negative bias and focused on the positive? How did you feel?

Is there a situation you are in that could benefit from more gratitude?

BRAINSTORM: Gratitude

Is anything too small to feel grateful for?

What do you feel grateful for?

How does it feel when someone shows they are grateful to you?

How does it feel to let someone know you are grateful to him or her?

BRAINSTORM: Optimism (helpful thinking)

Is optimism *always* realistic?

Could optimism ever be unrealistic or even dangerous?

When is optimism useful?

When isn't optimism useful?

Where does optimism fit into keeping things in perspective?

BRAINSTORM: Perspective

What is perspective?

What might make it difficult to keep things in perspective?

What might help to keep things in perspective?

High side (helpful thinking) and low side (unhelpful thinking): guide sheet

To explore how optimists and pessimists think, introduce the perspective of 'high side' and 'low side' using the guide sheet found at the end of this chapter.

When you're being optimistic (thinking on the high side), it's like standing on top of a mountain. You see and notice more. When you're being pessimistic (thinking on the low side), you see less and it's like standing in a valley. 'High side' thinking is helpful, 'low side' thinking is unhelpful. This doesn't mean that you ignore what is going wrong but it does mean that you focus on what is going well and what you can do about what is going wrong. Different ways of thinking can make a big difference to how you feel and what you might do when you're faced with your next challenge.

Role plays: high side and low side

Using the 'high side' (helpful thinking, optimistic) and 'low side' (unhelpful thinking, pessimistic) guide sheet, students can role play the following challenges and victories in pairs or small groups. They must consider a reaction if they had a 'high side' view and a reaction if they had a 'low side' view for each role play. Students can either present each role play twice – once showing a high side (optimistic) view and once showing a low side (pessimistic) view. Or, each partner in a pair can have fun where one is the optimist and the other a pessimist (then vice versa) and they debate how to look at the situation.

The reactions should show an understanding about the four kinds of thoughts shown in the guide sheet that optimists (high side, helpful thinkers) and pessimists (low side, unhelpful thinkers) express through challenges or victories. Remember this is not a problem-solving exercise – this is a perspective-building exercise. Students do not need to solve the problem – they need to consider different ways to look at what has happened.

Continue referring to 'high side/helpful thinking' and 'low side/unhelpful thinking' when students come across a difficulty where optimism and balanced perspective can make all the difference to what the solution might be. The more practice and processing they use around thinking styles, the more likely the skills will become engrained and come easily. Remind students that optimism is not about ignoring reality or what has gone wrong but it is about being solution-focused and keeping things in perspective.

Role plays about challenges for younger students

You have been dreaming of cookies all day. You come home from school and you open the kitchen cupboard. There are no cookies left.

You have been given a complete set of sports cards showing your favourite team. All the people in your class are looking at them. You go to the bathroom. When you come back, they are gone.

You love your new puppy so much. You gave it some chocolate and mum is angry. She said a puppy can get very sick if it eats chocolate.

Your best friend just ignored you when you said, 'hello'.

You are late for school because you fell off your bike on the way. The bell has gone.

Your lunchbox is missing from your bag. You feel sure you packed it this morning.

The school bell went five minutes ago. No one has come to pick you up. You can't find your brother or sister either.

Role plays about victories for younger students

You came first in the school marathon.

You were chosen for the lead in a drama performance.

You found part of a missing game.

You won the school raffle.

You are star of the day in your classroom.

You get chosen to look after the class pet over the school holidays.

You got all the answers right in your spelling test.

You are the first to test out the new microscope in science.

Role plays about challenges for older students

You can't find your mobile phone/tablet/laptop. You are sure you packed it this morning.

You are being bullied for the first time since you started at your new school.

You don't understand the new maths your teacher has just explained.

You have been asked to present a project you did well in at the school assembly but you feel shy about it.

You have been called into the principal's office unexpectedly.

You get home from school. Your dad said he'd be there when you got home. He isn't.

Your best friend just ignored you when you said, 'hi'.

Your teacher sees you arrive late for class and shakes their head with a smile.

Role plays about victories for older students

You came first in the National Maths challenge.

You won a bike in the school raffle.

You are invited to speak at the opening of a museum exhibition about your final year research into an extinct bird species. You are proud and excited.

You win every race at the swimming carnival.

You are selected as House Captain for your sports house team.

You get chosen to take the class pet (a carpet python) home over the holidays.

You get a huge applause from the school after doing a presentation at assembly.

You get invited to a party by someone who is really popular with everyone.

Your parents surprise you with a ticket to go away on a short holiday with your friend's family.

Moods and the low side

A short conversation with your students . . .

There are times when your thoughts and feelings run away from you and you can easily get stuck in low side/unhelpful thinking. Moods (how you feel) can change from one day to the next (and sometimes several times in one day!) Your mood changes because of lots of things. It can change when you're hungry, tired, sick, too busy, not busy enough, after too much TV or computer, or when something tough has happened to you. Moods can trick you into taking low side (unhelpful) views, so it is important to understand their place in how you see your life and the world.

Moods show themselves in lots of different feelings like sadness, boredom, fear, frustration and anger. If you are someone whose moods are sensitive and change a lot you might want to try some ACTIVE MOOD COMBAT! (See next activity.)

Active mood combat (AMC): guide sheet

Hand out the active mood combat guide sheet at the end of the chapter for students to explore what kind of activities they enjoy that might contribute to a balanced mood and perspective. Younger students can listen to the ideas and draw themselves engaging in a handful of energising activities. Let them know the importance of doing a variety of positive things every day to help keep their brains balanced and optimistic.

Mood check-in

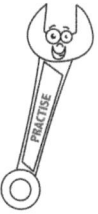

When you feel challenged or just plain grumpy, it can help to ask yourself, 'what am I feeling?' or 'what is my mood?' Just by naming your feeling or mood you often feel less worried by it. When you remember it's a mood steering your thoughts you can actually decide to ignore your thoughts until you check in and find your mood is more relaxed and happy. (You can get students to use this idea by asking them two or three times a day over a week to stop what they are doing and do a quick mood check-in.)

Gratitude journal

A short conversation with your students . . .

People often notice and pay more attention to what goes wrong around them. Other people's mistakes, their own mistakes, things that are broken, things they don't have – all use up more thinking time than is helpful for resilience and wellbeing. Gratitude journals are a great way to get you focused on what's going right from one day to the next. After a while your brain builds pathways for noticing what is going well and you naturally start focusing on positive and useful things rather than negative, unhelpful ones.

For older students, a journal can further extend the development of gratitude by getting your students to reflect on why the positive thing might have happened. It sounds easier than it is – especially on a regular day where there were no obvious highs or lows. A gratitude record sheet is found at the end of this chapter as an alternative to a separate gratitude journal.

21 day gratitude check-in

Hand out the '7 day gratitude record sheet' found at the end of this chapter. Each student will need three copies to complete the challenge.

After 21 days of consistent journaling, ask students to look over their journal and find gratitude patterns. Where does most of their gratitude come from? Family? Friends? Nature? Hobbies? Suggest they place their gratitude into categories. Allow them some time to do this and to enjoy the blessings in their lives. You might like to continue gratitude practice in your classroom through circle time where students can share one thing from their day they feel grateful for.

Hot and cold gratitude through empathy

Place your class into pairs and all go outside. Ask each pair to look out for things around them they feel grateful for. One at a time, one person in the pair identifies something they feel grateful for. They do not tell their partner what it is. The partner must then take a moment to empathise with the other person's sense of gratitude and try and guess what it is by walking towards it. Their partner calls out, 'warm, warmer, hot, hotter, on fire' if they are approaching it, and 'cold, colder, Antarctica' as they move further away from it. This is a fun way to see what other people feel gratitude for and provides an opportunity for perspective taking too.

Gratitude photo/illustration board

Allow students a week to think about what they are most grateful for – other than their family and friends. Ask them to photograph or illustrate it and post it in a designated place anonymously. Once all the students have contributed, make up a gratitude pin-up board. Let students know they have a few days to observe and think about what people have put up on the board. At the end of a school day, play some music and allow some time for students to take turns to guess who showed gratitude for what. This is a great activity in empathy and perspective taking and opens up new ways of finding gratitude by seeing what others are grateful for.

Sticky note gratitude day/week/month!

Provide each student with a sticky note per day with a classmate's name on it. Their goal is to write or draw something about that person that shows gratitude for who they are or something they did. Sticky notes (or small cards if easier) can be placed on each person's pigeon hole/desk/drawer/locker by the end of each day. If necessary keep a record of which child is showing gratitude for whom to make sure the task is carried out for all and no one is left out.

Thank a police, ambulance or fire department

Talk about how hard working and generous fire fighters and police officers are with their lives and time. As a class send them letters or drawings to express gratitude.

Gratitude role plays

Divide the group into pairs or small groups. Rather than providing prepared situations for gratitude role plays, the challenge is for each group to come up with a role play based on personal experiences where they felt gratitude for something another person did for them. Experiencing gratitude for others is important in all relationships and when it is noted and shared it builds deeper bonds (Gordon et al., 2012). Aim for at least one role play per group, but if there is time, allow each group member to come up with their own idea to role play.

Move mountains

Exercise is a well-known mood booster, balancing perspective and increasing optimism. Open a discussion about how our bodies are designed for keeping active. The human body has around 600 muscles that like to be kept active to maintain their strength and integrity. Our hearts need to pump blood around to oxygenate and detoxify our blood. Exercise is essential for our wellbeing!

The wants versus needs run

Having a good understanding about wants and needs makes a big difference to keeping perspective, being optimistic and feeling gratitude. Understanding there are plenty of *wants* in life but life can just as easily go on without them is important for developing good perspective. *Wants* fulfil our immediate desires – but don't make us happier in the long run. *Needs* have deeper purpose and meaning. Beyond the obvious needs of nutrition, shelter and health, there are other needs that increase our wellbeing and resilience such as purpose, connection and belonging.

Take the group to the playing field or gymnasium. Call out from the list below asking students to run from one end of the area to the other depending on whether they classify what you call out as a want or a need for wellbeing. Remind students a 'want' is something you would like but you can live without it and it won't affect your wellbeing much. A 'need' is also something you would like but you can't live without it and it increases your wellbeing when you do have it. Let the students know to follow their own instincts about what is a want or a need. There is not always a definitive answer.

Wants and needs for wellbeing

Water	Photographs
Mobile phone	Talent
Internet	Chocolate
Books	Skill
Love	Health
Friendship	Gratitude
Exercise	Integrity
Money	Goals
Food	Television
Sleep	Cake
Play	Cool clothes
Pets	Sport
Fun	Toys
Pocket money	Understanding
Education	Nature
Purpose	Bicycles
Family	Fans
Religion/spirituality	

Mountain pose

This energising yoga position can easily be done in the classroom. Yoga can help bring the opposite feeling of the stressful fight or flight reaction and is excellent for wellbeing (Bhattacharjee and Arora, 2008). If your group shows interest in the poses and you can factor time in to engage in them, try adding one new pose a week. By the end of the school year you might have the most relaxed class in the school!

High side and low side relay

This works easiest with two leaders who can then listen to each team's answers.

Divide the group into two teams. One team is the 'high side' and the other team is the 'low side'. Place one half of each team on one side of the court and the other half of that team on the opposite side. Then, beside the team place the opposition. Provide the 'high side' and the 'low side' each with a baton. Read out the statements below. The 'high side' must come up with one optimistic response to your statement and the 'low side' must come up with one pessimistic statement in order to move. You might find it easier to do this with another leader so you can each be responsible for listening to one team or the other. The game continues until one team has relayed all their players.

Statements

- I've broken my leg and it's sports day tomorrow.
- I've lost my mum's favourite scarf.
- Our team lost the soccer season.
- I am so thirsty.
- I have been banned from watching television for a week!
- My parents are going away without us and we have to stay with my granny.
- I left my homework at home.
- It is pouring with rain.
- It is so hot outside.

- The class is watching a movie together that I have seen five times already.
- There is a new child in my class joining today.
- I have to start at a new school.
- My family is moving house to a new area.
- Sports practice is cancelled tonight.
- The canteen has just run out of donuts. I always get a donut!
- I won the raffle for a bike that is too small for me.
- The vegetables I planted at home just don't seem to be growing.
- I need to wear glasses for reading.
- I am really sick and have to cancel my birthday party tomorrow.
- A lost kitten is on my doorstep.
- There is no room left to write in a group card for my best friend's birthday.
- My school uniforms blew off the line last night and are completely covered in mud. I have no spares.
- I have finally saved up for a gaming system and the store has run out completely.
- I didn't get any sleep last night and I'm exhausted.
- My best friend is leaving our school.
- My best friend isn't at school today.
- I have a drama exam today and I forgot all about it.
- We are going on a school excursion to a place I go to every weekend with my family.
- I'm coming last in this relay!

The high side (optimism) walk

Take your students on a walk around the neighbourhood (or school yard) with a small paper bag for each child. Remind them to breathe in deeply as they walk and to feel their bodies move as they go around. Ask them to look around and place up to five things in their bag that for them represent optimism. Be prepared for a class discussion about why certain things were collected. Some students will see things that represent optimism that can't be brought back in a bag. These can be reflected on during the discussion time.

Optimism bake off

Set a homework task of students finding the most optimistic saying they have ever heard. Provide all students with a piece of baking paper and ask them to write their saying on it. Collect all the sayings and enjoy a bread roll/cupcake bake off where optimistic sayings are baked inside each roll/cake for students to be surprised with at lunchtime together.

Weekly challenge

This week's challenge is to observe family and friends. Listen out for 'high side – helpful' talk and 'low side – unhelpful' talk. Your goal is to decide who you know that shows the most optimism (or 'high side' talk). Make them a certificate of optimism with examples of their optimism. Bring it in to show your teacher and then enjoy handing it to your optimism mentor.

Parent tips

Maintain a balanced perspective

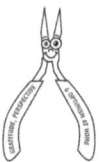

Young people are keen observers. When they see someone they love facing a strong emotion such as shock, frustration or disappointment their love for that person puts them on high alert. What will mum do now she didn't get that job she really wanted? What will dad do now that person opened their car door hard and put a dent in his car? What will the adult do? What will the adult say? Parents and teachers carry a responsibility as role models to young people. As young people see you maintaining perspective, being optimistic and expressing gratitude they are more likely to take these methods of thinking on – especially when they see how much better things turn out when you approach life this way.

Give thanks

Think about the last time you did something nice for someone. How did you feel when you heard the words, 'thank you?' How would you have felt if those words never came? 'Thank you' can never be overestimated. It adds to the glue of all relationships. Use the words 'thank you' and 'I appreciate you' often. When your child helps out, it is more meaningful to say 'thank you' than 'good boy/girl'. Let your children see you being thankful every day for all your blessings. Sunshine, rain, learning something new, a flower in the garden, humour, a hot shower, health, each other, a meal – there is usually so much to be thankful for. When someone does something for you, no matter how small, always thank them, using their name if you know it, and be generous with your smile. As your children see and hear you express gratitude as a daily habit, they'll pick up on that. Thank the waiter, the store clerk, the electrician, the party hosts, the bank teller, the doctor, the receptionist, the teacher, the cleaner, the librarian, the person who moves out of the way as you walk through – say thanks to everyone!

Consider reducing material possessions – even by a fraction

Ever watched a child with too many presents on Christmas morning? Sometimes Christmas morning feels like a let-down – the build-up was more exciting! Anticipating what might come is fun! Not knowing is fun! Getting something you've wanted for a long time is fun! Getting lots of things you've wanted for anywhere between a day and a few weeks is not as much fun. Watch how your child receives a gift. Do they unwrap it and discard it only to open the next one and repeat? Or do they open their gift and marvel there is something inside they've been saving for or have wanted for months (maybe even years!) When you receive something you've been working hard for, you naturally feel gratitude. Children who are allowed to buy a small toy or eat a treat every time they enter a store or go on a family outing may feel less grateful. This is especially true if the child hasn't had to earn or save money to buy his or her *wants*. Saying 'no' is always harder than saying 'yes', but it shows strong boundaries, good impulse control and a value in each other more than things.

Write thank you notes

After a birthday or holiday, sit down with your children and write a note to give thanks. The note doesn't have to be long. If your child can't write yet, you write the note and let them write their name or draw a picture showing what they're thankful for. Modern-day technology means older children might be in the habit of sending text messages and emails. If they are not likely to spend the time writing a letter it is much better to send a message through media like this than not send thanks at all.

Stop and smell the roses

Remember when your children were babies and toddlers and everything was new? They would marvel at everything and focus all their attention on it. There's so much joy to be had by stopping and enjoying what's in front of you. Look deeply at a flower; notice its parts, its colour, and its smell. Lie on the grass and look between its blades. Tiny bugs, new shoots, moist dirt. Cloud watch. Stop and watch a caterpillar. Be curious about it. Where is it going? What will it do next? Take slow walks where it is okay to just stop and notice something. Give time to examine deeply and thoughtfully. Nature is full of gifts and surprises.

Sing and be silly

For many of us, singing and being silly kind of go hand in hand. If you can't hit the note – don't worry – that's where silly comes in! Singing can be such a positive thing to do. When you sing you feel joy and that joy is passed on to those around you. Share family songs you all enjoy together and immerse yourself in family singalongs. If you're not into the singing side of things, then play happy music and enjoy someone else's singing!

Sing songs with a positive message

Every now and again when you just can't reach your child and they are feeling down, muck around a little and sing a song. They may laugh or they may throw something at you. Either way it's worth a shot! Songs with a positive message include, 'Don't Worry, Be Happy' (Bobby McFerrin), 'Happy' (Pharrel Williams) and 'Always Look on the Bright Side of Life' (Eric Idle).

Keep a family gratitude journal for 21 days

Earlier in this chapter your child was taught how to use a gratitude journal. Using the framework offered, consider doing the same for your family.

The difference will be that gratitude will not focus on individuals, but it will focus on the family as a unit. What happened today for the family to feel grateful? On some days you can extend by adding individual family members too of course.

Show optimism

Demonstrate a belief that things will work out, or that everything happens for a reason. When difficult times challenge you, while it can be appropriate to share your feelings of disappointment or frustration, make the focus on what you're going to do about it. If you don't like your job and your child knows it, show them you plan to seek out new opportunities or learn new skills. If changing jobs is not an option then show them how you choose to spend your free time doing things that are positive. Try and avoid your child thinking bad things happen to good people and that there is not much you can do about it. An attitude like this is a great catalyst for poor perspective, pessimism and losing a sense of gratitude.

FROM THE LOW SIDE (UNHELPFUL THINKING) TO THE HIGH SIDE (HELPFUL THINKING)

"Yippee, it's awesome up here! I can handle anything! I see clearly and it's looking good"

"Oooooh it's so bad down here. Things don't ever work out. I can't see anything good. It's all bad"

Thinking on the **LOW SIDE** is when you notice everything that's wrong. It's like standing low in a valley and you can't see a way out. This is **UNHELPFUL THINKING**. Thinking on the **HIGH SIDE** is when you keep things in perspective. It's like standing on top of a mountain and getting a clear view about what's going well. This is **HELPFUL THINKING**.

HIGH SIDE (HELPFUL THINKING) when something goes WRONG sounds like this:	HIGH SIDE (HELPFUL THINKING) when something goes RIGHT sounds like this:
"This problem won't last forever."	"Things can only get better!"
"I can do something about this." It's one thing - not everything ."	"I love my life! Things just turn out well!"
"There are lots of great people and things around me. This is difficult but there's good things too."	"I am so lucky!"

LOW SIDE (UNHELPFUL THINKING) when something goes WRONG sounds like this:	LOW SIDE (UNHELPFUL THINKING) when something goes RIGHT sounds like this:
"Bad things keep happening to ME!"	"Something will go wrong soon"
"Its always bad for me"	"It was just luck. It won't happen again"
"Everything in my life goes wrong for me!"	"This is just one thing that turned out well - everything else will go badly."

ACTIVE MOOD COMBAT

Circle 5 things or more you like doing from the list. Keeping active, adventurous and involved in different things is important for your wellbeing.

ACTIVE MOOD COMBAT TO CALM LOW MOODS

- Exercise
- Laugh
- A change of scenery
- Pretend you're a tourist and see your city from new eyes
- Dance
- Do something kind for someone else
- Remember a favourite place or time
- Gratitude - find things you feel grateful for
- Lie under a tree and breathe deeply

- Talk to someone
- Do something you love
- Cloud watch
- Garden
- Go for a bike ride
- Breathe deeply and slowly
- Listen to music
- Cook
- Draw
- Meditate

If you are having trouble handling your moods tell someone you trust. Low moods can take over. Remember the old saying,

"A problem shared is a problem halved"∗

7 DAY GRATITUDE RECORD SHEET

Use this record sheet to draw or write three things that went well that you are grateful for each day. At the end of the seven days post this up and celebrate it together with others. Try and keep this going for at least 21 days.

Day 1			
Day 2			
Day 3			
Day 4			
Day 5			
Day 6			
Day 7			

"Wake at dawn with a winged heart and give thanks for another day of loving" Kahlil Gibran

Reference list

Bhattacharjee, J. and Arora, S. 2008. 'Modulation of Immune Responses in Stress by Yoga'. *International Journal of Yoga* Vol. 1 No. 2, pp. 45–55.

Baumeister, R. et al. 2001. 'Bad Is Stronger Than Good'. *Review of General Psychology* Vol. 5 No. 4, pp. 323–370. doi:10.1037/1089-2680.5.4.323.

Cacioppo, J. et al. 2007. *Handbook of Psychophysiology*. Cambridge: Cambridge University Press.

Emmons, R. and McCullough, M. 2003. 'Counting Blessings Versus Burdens: An Experimental Investigation of Gratitude and Subjective Well-Being in Daily Life'. *Journal of Personality and Social Psychology* Vol. 84 No. 2, pp. 377–389.

Gordon, A. M. et al. 2012. 'To Have and to Hold: Gratitude Promotes Relationship Maintenance in Intimate Bonds'. *Journal of Personality and Social Psychology* Vol. 103 No. 2, pp. 257–274.

Rozin, P. et al. 2001. 'Negativity Bias, Negativity Dominance, and Contagion'. *Personality and Social Psychology Review* Vol. 5 No. 4, pp. 296–320.

Rubin, G. 2011. *The Happiness Project: Or, Why I Spent a Year Trying to Sing in the Morning, Clean My Closets, Fight Right, Read Aristotle, and Generally Have More Fun*. New York: HarperCollins.

Seligman, M. 2007. *The Optimistic Child: A Proven Program to Safeguard Children Against Depression and Build Lifelong Resilience*. Sydney: Houghton Mifflin.

Seligman, M. 2011 *Flourish: A Visionary New Understanding of Happiness and Wellbeing*. New York: Simon and Schuster.

2 Knowing your values and sticking to them

Be yourself; everyone else is already taken.
Oscar Wilde

Introduction for teachers and health professionals

Authenticity or living according to your values supports healthy psychological functioning and positive subjective wellbeing (Goldman and Kernis, 2002).

Working out what your values are and sticking to them with integrity is not always easy. The complex interaction between genetics, nature and nurture, biology, neurology, temperament and environment can all affect individual values.

To look within and find what matters most to you can also lead to self-discovery around personal strengths and difficulties. To live by your values it helps to be authentic and this means acknowledging your less desirable traits. Some find this easier than others. For many young people their imperfections and mistakes are seen as personal shortcomings rather than a natural part of the human experience. This can lead to higher levels of stress and lower levels of resilience and wellbeing, as they put their energy into keeping this information from others in order to appear somewhat perfect on the outside. The support and encouragement of others can make a difference to how smoothly a young person will travel along this road, especially when coming to terms with having different values from their friends or family.

This chapter helps students understand their values, to help them further develop authenticity and integrity. It encourages them to focus on their strengths while acknowledging their difficulties, understanding that there is no such thing as a perfect person.

Explanation for all students

Values are things you believe are important and fair. A value has to feel right for you and match the way you think and feel about life. For example, if one of the things you really believe in (value) is kindness, you don't need anyone to keep reminding you to be kind, you are kind because kindness feels right and natural to you. It's easy. There are lots of other values like honesty, empathy, generosity, equality, excellence, peace, freedom and spirituality.

Once you know what your values are, it helps if you live by them and stick to them. This can be really hard if your values are different from your friends' values or your family's values. To stand by your values and be honest about how you live is a value called 'integrity'. Integrity sets you up to get along well with others and to feel pride in who you are. Integrity is about being truthful about who you are and what you do. Having integrity lets you be 'authentic' – the real you. When you are authentic you show people who you really are and you don't try to be someone else.

Someone with values and integrity:

Birke Baehr: health and nutrition advocate

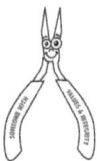

When Birke Baehr was a little boy he wanted to be a National League Football player. Then something happened. When he was just 10 years old he learnt food was not always what it seemed. Some foods looked good at first but were actually genetically modified or covered in chemicals to make them last longer. Birke learnt soon enough how this could make people sick, yet food was supposed to bring people health and nutrition. When he found out how some big companies advertise their unhealthy food in packaging that makes children really want to eat it – using ideas like putting toys inside the packages, Birke knew something had to change. When he realised how most people had no idea what they were eating, it went against his **values**. His strong character and **integrity** led him to find out more about what was going on and TEDx gave him the chance to speak about his ideas to his first big audience. As the youngest ever TEDx speaker to date he has had almost 2,000 views of his very powerful and passionate presentation. Check it out at www.ted.com/speakers/birke_baehr. Birke no longer wants to be a National League footballer; he wants to be an organic farmer and continue speaking to audiences around the globe about the value of knowing more about what you eat. Birke simply states:

> *Eat good food and you stay healthy. Eat bad food and you get sick . . . so next time you're at the grocery store, think local, choose organic, know your farmer and know your food.*

GROUP BRAINSTORM: Tuning in to feelings and values: following your gut feelings

The central concept is feelings and values.

'Who has done something that didn't feel right but did it anyway?'

'Why might people do something that doesn't feel right?'

'What does it feel like to do something that doesn't feel right?'

'Who noticed feelings in their stomach or chest?'

'What kind of thoughts do people have when they do something that doesn't feel right?'

'What about doing something that feels right even though other people don't agree? Has anyone ever done that?'

'Why might people do something that feels right even though their friends tease them about it or disagree?'

'What does it feel like when you have the courage to do what feels right?'

'How does your body feel when you do something right?'

'What kind of thoughts do you have when you do something right?'

Gut feelings

A short conversation with your students . . .

When you do something that doesn't feel right, you might get a funny feeling in your stomach or chest. People call this a 'gut feeling'. It's your body's way of warning you something isn't right. When you get feelings like that, it is a good idea to check in with yourself and ask, 'Am I being true?' If you are not being true, ask yourself, 'How can I be true to myself now?' Sometimes you need to talk to a trusted friend or adult when you find yourself getting gut feelings that make you feel uncomfortable. Friends and carers are there to help and support you.

Finding my values: worksheet

Provide students with the values worksheet and guide sheet found at the end of this chapter. Remind students a value is something they believe in and when they use that value they feel good about it. Ask your students to read the values carefully (or for younger students, slowly read them out and offer a shorter list). Allow students a few minutes to think about the list and, if you wish, let them discuss the values in small groups. Challenge students to choose five values that truly reflect who they are and record them on their 'Finding my values' worksheet along with the thoughts and feelings they experience when using that value. Remind them this activity is about answering for yourself and not what you think your teacher, parents, or friends think you should answer. Another option is to dedicate a value for each day until you get through the list. This way the class has each value as a theme and tries the value out, developing a stronger understanding of whether or not the value feels authentic to them. After exploring values deeper this way, you can then return to the guide sheet and worksheet.

'Who am I?' (for older students), and 'Me and my favourite things' (for younger students): worksheets

Provide students with the worksheet 'Who am I?' or 'Me and my favourite things' depending on age and ability. Allow at least 20–30 minutes to complete the exercise. The worksheets provide students with an opportunity to further explore their interests and values.

BRAINSTORM

Read the following quote to your class and brainstorm what it might mean:

Honesty and transparency make you vulnerable, but be honest and transparent anyway.

Mother Theresa

Differences in values

A short conversation with your students . . .

It can be frustrating when one of your friends or family sees things differently from you. Their values appear unusual and sometimes you can't even begin to understand them. Respect is about accepting differences in values even if you don't understand or like them. Everyone has a right to choose their own values, feel heard and be understood.

You can only be in control of yourself. Your wellbeing grows when you focus on your own values and avoid trying to control other people's (or wish theirs were more like yours). Feeling frustrated by the differences between you and other people takes up a lot of energy. Your resilience is stronger when you put your energy into things you can change. You can put your own values to work and maybe even make the world a better place!

Other people's values: reflective thinking journal activity

Display or read out the list of values from the guide sheet at the end of this chapter. Ask students to work out which value they believe in the least and to write it down in their journal. Ask the following questions and ask them to record the answers in their journal:

Who do you know who might live by this value?

Why do you think they feel good when they live by this value?

Do you ever use this value?

How is this value different from your strongest value?

How is this value the same as your strongest value?

Can you be friends with someone who has a value you do not value?

Group discussion about honesty and integrity

(Facilitators might want to raise their hand as well to show students their willingness to be authentic and honest.)

Have you ever done the wrong thing?

Have you ever tried to hide something you have said or done?

How did it feel when you did the wrong thing?

Did you ever hide the truth about something you did only to be found out later?

Did you learn anything from it? If so, what?

Values for my resilience and wellbeing guide sheet: how will you be remembered?

Provide students with the 'Values for my resilience and wellbeing' guide sheet found at the end of this chapter to help students understand integrity, authenticity and respect.

The self-integrity oath: self-reflection journal activity

Many clubs and associations have some kind of oath about how their members should behave to uphold the standards of the group. An integrity oath is a promise to yourself to aim high to follow your values and do what you can to make your own life and other people's lives better. Students can learn a lot about themselves and extend their knowledge about their core values by writing their own integrity oath.

When writing an oath, ask your students to say what they WILL do rather than what they WILL NOT do. For example instead of, 'I will not tell lies', the oath would read, 'I will be truthful'. The oaths can later be made into a class poster to follow throughout the school year, or combined together to make a class oath for all.

Framework for a self-integrity oath

I will try my best to be true to my family, my neighbourhood and my school.

I will respect everything and everyone around me.

I will make the world a better place.

Encourage students to focus on what they believe in and what is important to them, otherwise the oath will be difficult to stick to and will lose authenticity.

Repairing lost integrity

A short conversation with your students . . .

While you're learning about friendships and how to get along with others, you are bound to make mistakes along the way. No one is perfect and if you don't make mistakes it's fair to say you're probably avoiding doing a whole bunch of stuff you could end up enjoying. Mistakes happen to everyone and they give your brain a chance to feel challenged and learn something new. Your brain will appreciate these opportunities for growth and so will you.

What happens when you stop listening to your values and someone else gets hurt?

Role plays: repairing lost integrity

Role play the following scenario using the three different reasons for your actions. Some students will happily create their own scenarios, and allow this where possible.

Role play scenario

A person you don't know well asks you to play with them at lunch. You answer, 'yes' and agree to meet them on the bench. You don't show up. Talk to the person using the framework below and cover three reasons per scenario using the framework: 'I'm sorry that I didn't meet you . . . I (reason). You must have felt (feeling). How can I make it better?'

REASON 1:   You didn't really want to play with them in the first place so you hid from them.

REASON 2:   You forgot.

REASON 3:   You told your friends about a new person joining at lunch-time and they said, 'No! We already have too many people in our group.'

What would you do if no one was watching?

Allow the class a couple of minutes to imagine themselves in the classroom – alone. Ask them what would they do? How might they feel while they were doing it? How might they feel afterwards? Would they use the time usefully – or would they use it cheekily? Allow this discussion to be fun and light-hearted. Some students will enjoy fabricating over-the-top stories. Have fun with this activity and be sure you take part as well!

Role plays: truth and lies

The following role plays are best done in groups of three. Only the students performing will be told who is telling the truth in the story.

Following the role play, ask the audience how they knew who was being truthful and who was lying. Ask students which student they would feel more comfortable being and why.

Friends argue over who was last to have a set of misplaced sports trading cards.

The teacher notices some money missing from her handbag. She calls on two students who were seen coming out of the classroom during lunch.

An unkind note has been found in the classroom about a student. The handwriting is a good match for two students in the class. The principal takes the students into her office to discuss the matter.

A group of three friends have an argument over something. The angriest group member storms off and tells the teacher the other two students have been spreading rumours about her. The group is brought together to discuss what happened.

The answers to tomorrow's test are missing from the teacher's desk. Two students claim their innocence to the teacher.

BRAINSTORM: What makes integrity so challenging sometimes?

Most people know what is right and fair and want to do the right thing. So, why do people sometimes upset or hurt others? Why do people not always stand up for what they believe in? Why do some people hide the truth?

The link between integrity, respect and reputation

A short conversation with your students . . .

> *Live in such a way that should anyone speak badly of you, no one would believe them.*
>
> (unknown source)

On the whiteboard, write C. S Lewis's quote on integrity, 'Integrity is doing the right thing even when no one is watching.' Ask students to discuss whether there are often times when no one is watching.

The reality is, in a community, people can't help but notice and hear what others are doing and saying around them. Whether it is fair or not, people often make judgements about what they notice other people doing. By living with integrity, respecting others, and themselves, students have the best chance of building and maintaining a good reputation. End by asking your students, 'how will you be remembered?'

Group discussion questions about integrity, respect and reputation

Have you ever heard someone say something bad about someone you know?

Did you believe what you heard?

Why do some rumours feel more believable than others?

Have you ever been the subject of a rumour? If so, how did it feel?

Do rumours affect someone's reputation?

Have you ever said or done something that has upset others?

What makes a reputation?

Can a reputation be changed?

'If it was up to me' worksheet

Hand out the 'If it was up to me' worksheet at the end of this chapter. This worksheet is designed to encourage students to think about the ways they would use choice and autonomy based on their values.

'Things bigger than me' survey

Hand out the 'Things bigger than me' survey at the end of this chapter. Happiness and wellbeing can increase when we find value in and become involved in something bigger outside of ourselves (Sagiv and Schwartz, 2000;

Seligman, 2011). This survey is a great way to help students explore ways in which they can be of service and contribute to others.

Creating a vision statement

After completing the survey you can extend the activity by encouraging students to summarise their values and ability to be of service by creating a personal vision statement on a blank piece of paper. Vision statements should reflect what is important to them in their life right now. To help them get started, display the sample vision statements below (younger students can draw their vision and purpose instead of writing).

> For someone whose vision and purpose is to improve the lives of others:
>
> 'I will be a living example of what it is to be kind and understanding. I will generously contribute to enrich the lives of my family, friends and those around me.'

> For someone whose vision and purpose is to protect animals:
>
> 'I will seek to support the needs of those who have no voice, the animals in this world. I will seek to improve their wellbeing by respecting and caring for their needs.'

> For someone whose vision and purpose is to care for the environment:
>
> 'I will touch the earth gently to help it grow. I will encourage others to do the same.'

A project with a purpose

Set a project for students to work through over a reasonable period of time (up to a full school term is ideal). Ask students to seek to find out as much as possible about something they showed interest in on their 'Things bigger than me' survey. Use the goal setting worksheet from Chapter 8 to encourage students to explain their interest and how they might follow it up using the steps framework. Students can then create a short video clip to summarise what they learnt about, and present this to the class.

I can't be anyone but me: exploring fingerprints

Take a print of every student's fingers and thumbs on a card, with enough room to write a few words beside each print. You may choose to take prints from one or both hands. After discussing how fingerprints are individual and allowing students to compare their own fingerprints with those of their classmates, link this to our unique personalities. Next to each thumb and fingerprint ask students to write down something positive and unique about themselves that sets them apart from their family, friends or community.

An avalanche of lies

Young children can become quite competent at deception from around the age of 5 (Lewis, 1993). Often lies are to do with staying out of trouble, but at other times they are an extension of a child's imagination and they enjoy telling the tale to an audience. It can also be hard for them sometimes to tell the difference between what is reality and what is imagination. This stage of deception is a normal and important part of development (Oswalt et al., 2008).

Older children from around the age of 7 can find themselves caught up in a lie while defending an action. The first lie often happens on impulse and they then need to keep the story going to stay out of trouble. While all children benefit from clear boundaries around the importance of telling the truth, young people need understanding and encouragement to learn to be more honest.

Playing around with truth and lies in games can be a fun way to explore this concept openly. While spending time with your students on another task, interrupt what you are doing and start pointing out things that aren't there, like, 'Hey, look at that baby riding a donkey outside the classroom.' You should get a laugh. A few minutes later, point out another absurd 'observation', like, 'Hey, look at that! The donkey is now riding the baby.' How many laughs did you get this time? Repeat a couple of times more, again paying attention to how much the laughter is reducing. Once you can see you are no longer getting a laugh, open a discussion around telling lies – even just to be funny. Ask the students the following questions:

Was it funny the first time I pointed out the baby and the donkey thing?

Was it as funny the second time?

What about by the third or fourth time? How were you feeling by then?

How would you feel if I said things that weren't true all the time?

If I made up things all the time, would you trust me? (Younger students would benefit from a short explanation about what trust is.)

Is there any danger in telling lies – even just really silly and small ones?

Valuing differences: celebrating diversity

Cultures around the world have many ways to acknowledge religion, spirituality and tradition. A calendar showing the different celebrations around the world based on your group of students can be a great way to focus on values and diversity.

You can add to the calendar through student research and acknowledge as many traditions as you like throughout the year. This can be as simple as sharing a story from another country, showing respect for the day, or you can extend this further with food from the country, dress-up days, class presentations and so forth. Teaching young people early on about the value of diversity builds character and opens opportunities for them in their relationships and understanding of others that will increase their wellbeing.

Weekly challenge: standing up for your values

Sticking to your values and standing up for what you believe in might feel strange at first, but the more you do it the better it feels. This week, see if you can say or do something that shows your true self and values. If you want to go a step further – defend someone you know or someone famous that you admire but that other people don't like.

Other ways to show integrity and use your values:

Admit when you are wrong.
Learn from mistakes.
Work hard.
Forgive.
Tell the truth.
Say 'no' when you don't want to do something.

Parent tips for developing values that encourage integrity and authenticity

Identify your family values

One of the easiest ways to figure out what your boundaries are as a parent is to work out what your key values are. Once everyone in the family acknowledges and understands what these values are, you can display them where everyone can see them. When someone crosses a boundary that does not respect the family value, you can kindly remind him or her, 'in our family honesty is important'. This keeps boundaries around behaviour clear and consistent.

Create a family storybook

Try starting a scrapbook that becomes a collection of your family's stories. You can go back to previous generations with stories of love, courage and loss, giving your children insight into where they came from and what previous members of their family experienced. Add stories from the past and present day and keep building. When family life gets busy and everyone needs a recharge, pull it out and enjoy reflecting back on these treasured tales.

Encourage respectful behaviour and communication

When your child, asking for something, speaks to you in a way that is not respectful, let them know you will give them a moment to reframe their request. If you do not like the way your child is speaking to you, try not to fall into the trap of giving them what they are asking for at that time. Expect high (but reasonable) standards around manners, attitude and tone of voice.

Avoid hiding your challenges

Although children should not be exposed to information about larger family stressors such as conflict or financial insecurity, it is important for you to model that you experience challenges too. Like everyone, you have strengths and weaknesses, joys and sorrows, achievements and failures. Vulnerability and uncertainty are sometimes just part of life. When you create a space for understanding this and share your journey (where appropriate) with your children, you show them your courage to live with values and authenticity.

Say 'sorry'

Few things make a person feel more vulnerable and more authentic than taking responsibility for something they have done wrong. Saying sorry is an important skill. When you have said or done something that in retrospect was unjust, show courage and tell your child you're sorry.

Walk the talk

Children are sensitive to hypocrisy. If you hold a strong boundary in your home about telling the truth then make sure you tell the truth yourself. Children are often watching and listening and they are the first to notice contradictions in what we say and do. If you want your children to build strong character and values, live the life of the person you want them to become.

Help children find their own interests and talents

One of the hardest things when you're a parent is seeing untapped potential in your child. You see how talented or skilled they are in a particular area and know they could turn it into something useful but your child has no interest in developing that skill. Many people revert to using a natural born talent because it appears to be the easiest thing to do. If you push your child to follow a natural skill they have no passion for, they are likely to become unmotivated and unhappy. Just because you're good at something doesn't mean you should pursue it. Listen as much as possible to what your child feels passionate about so you can help guide your child towards reaching their true potential.

Keep an eye on social media

Social media with all its benefits adds challenges to living a life of authenticity. Young people using social media are often bombarded throughout their day with photos of friends having fun, wearing cool new clothes, eating food they wish they were eating and looking at the camera as if not a moment of their life is challenging, mundane or idle. How on earth can young people let themselves be vulnerable and authentic with images like that around them? Young people have an inherent need to fit in with their peers, in whatever form that might take, and not feeling like you fit in can build stress and reduce resilience.

Educating and preparing young people with knowledge and skills about social media *before* they are users themselves is a good approach, since this is the best time to catch their attention, instead of waiting until they are engrossed in the experience. If they enter the world of social media with accurate information they are more likely to absorb its benefits. It can be helpful for young people to know nobody is happy all the time. Life can be mundane, challenging, unrewarding and repetitive. Sometimes life is full of sadness and disappointment. Excitement, success, adventure and happiness co-exist with these more challenging emotions, and when young people are given the skills to understand them their wellbeing and resilience increase. When young people fully understand that what they see on television and social media can sometimes lack authenticity, they can continue their journey towards being themselves, whoever that might be.

Celebrate cultural diversity

Introduce your child to music, stories, clothing and foods from a wide range of cultures. Take them to culture and art shows to show the diversity of people and places. Watch your family wellbeing increase as you learn new things together and add cultural traditions to part of the celebrations and rituals of your own family.

Sew a 'family values blanket' or make a poster

This allows an opportunity for shared creativity as well as focusing on values. Together as a family, brainstorm what values are held within the family. Seek to find common threads amongst individual values in order to connect them together. Aim to create a blanket or poster that represents your family values, and display it as a reminder of what you seek to live by.

FINDING MY VALUES

Write a value you believe in inside the rectangular box. Write the thoughts you have when you are using that value inside the thinking bubble. Write the feelings you get when you are using that value inside the heart.

VALUES GUIDE SHEET

VALUES

Caring (you care about other people/animals/belongings)

Compassion (you have empathy and want to help others)

Persistence (you work hard and don't give up)

Aim high (you do your best in everything)

Fair (you follow rules and treat people fairly)

Equality (you feel all people are equal no matter what their gender, religion, values or culture)

Manners (being polite and saying 'please' and 'thank you' are important to you)

Justice (you care about what is right and fair)

Freedom (you feel people have the right to be able to walk, live, play and learn freely)

Honesty (you tell the truth)

Integrity (you are true to yourself and act honestly)

Respect (you see yourself and other people as important even when their thoughts and feelings
are different to yours)

Responsibility (you take responsibility for your actions and you are trustworthy)

Understanding (you don't judge others, you try to understand them)

Cultural equality (you believe people from all cultures are equally important)

Kindness (you believe in doing kind things that help or make others feel good)

Service to others (you believe in volunteering your time to make the world a better place)

WHO AM I?

Name: _____

If I had to give away everything except one thing, this is what I would keep and why: _____
_____
_____
_____

Two people (or groups of people) I need most in my life and why:

1. _____
_____

2. _____
_____

Something I love doing - time flies when I'm doing it: _____
_____
_____

Three things I care about:

1. _____
_____

2. _____
_____

3. _____
_____

I can really imagine myself being a _____ when I grow up.
_____

One thing in my life I wish I could change: _____
_____
_____
_____

_____

ME AND MY FAVOURITE THINGS

1. Here I am when I am an adult, doing a job I really enjoy

2. Here I am with my favourite toy/thing to do

3. Here I am with something I really care about

4. Here I am in the 'flow' doing my hobby/something I love doing

VALUES FOR MY RESILIENCE AND WELLBEING

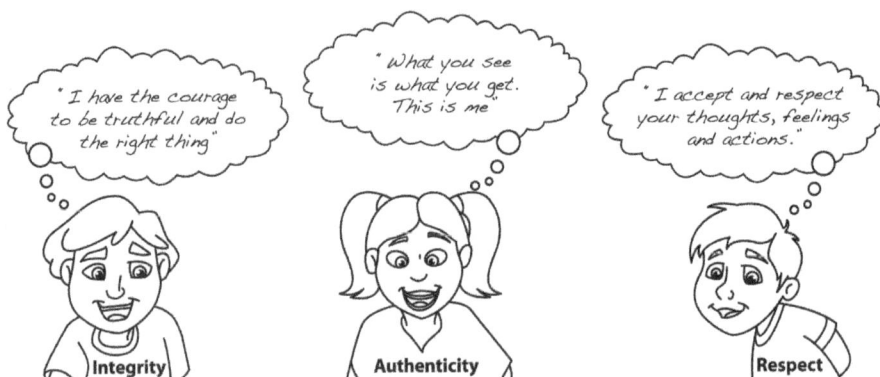

> "I have the courage to be truthful and do the right thing"

Integrity

> "What you see is what you get. This is me"

Authenticity

> "I accept and respect your thoughts, feelings and actions."

Respect

HOW WILL YOU BE REMEMBERED?

Step 1: INTEGRITY (BE HONEST)

Live an honest life. Have the courage to do the right thing even if other people don't agree.
'Integrity is always doing the right thing. Even when no one is watching.' (C.S. Lewis)

Step 2. AUTHENTICITY (BE TRUE)

Live the life you believe in. Stick to your values. Be yourself.

Step 3. RESPECT (BE UNDERSTANDING AND ACCEPTING)

Live in a way that is not harmful to yourself, harmful to others or harmful to the world.
Try to understand and respect other people's thoughts, feelings and opinions.

IF IT WAS UP TO ME

(A brainstorm/group discussion for younger students)

If it was up to me, the first lesson on a Monday morning would be: _____

_____

_____

If it was up to me every day our class would: _____

_____

_____

_____

If it was up to me the teacher's main job in the classroom other than teaching would be: _____

_____

_____

_____

If it was up to me the food in the tuck shop would be: _____

_____

_____

If it was up to me if someone behaved badly in the classroom the teacher would: _____

_____

_____

_____

If it was up to me when someone had trouble learning they could: _____

_____

_____

_____

If it was up to me lessons would be made more interesting by: _____

_____

_____

_____

THINGS BIGGER THAN ME SURVEY

People care about themselves and the people they love. Loving and caring for yourself and the people important to you strengthens your wellbeing. You are also capable of showing care towards people you don't know. When caring like this matches your values, you feel good and build your wellbeing and resilience. Circle what you care about below.

Freedom from hunger

Animal protection

Homelessness

Wildlife rescue

Clean parks and playgrounds

Education for all children

Connecting the elderly to communities

Health care for all

Literacy (all children having the chance to learn to read and write)

A cleaner environment

Curing serious illnesses

Clean drinking water in developing countries

Refugees

Wildlife protection

Reference list

Goldman, B. and Kernis, M. 2002. 'The Role of Authenticity in Healthy Psychological Functioning and Subjective Well-Being'. *Annals of the American Psychotherapy Association* Vol. 5 No. 6.

Lewis, M. 1993. 'The Development of Deception'. In Lewis, M. and Saarni, C., *Lying and Deception in Everyday Life*. New York: Guilford Press, pp. 90–105.

Oswalt, A., Staats Reiss, N. and Dombeck, M. 2008. 'Disorders and Issues of Child Development and Parenting: Lying in Early Childhood'. Accessed Online: www.mentalhelp.net.

Sagiv, L. and Schwartz, S. 2000. 'Value Priorities and Subjective Well-Being: Direct Relations and Congruity Effects'. *European Journal of Social Psychology* Vol. 30, pp. 177–198.

Seligman, M. 2011. *Flourish: A Visionary New Understanding of Happiness and Well-Being*. New York: Simon and Schuster.

3 Community and connection
The importance of empathy and belonging in relationships

I don't like that man. I must get to know him better.
Abraham Lincoln

Introduction for teachers and health professionals

Being surrounded by people you feel safe and comfortable with, and connected to, provides a strong foundation for confidence and wellbeing (Diener and Seligman, 2004). A community is where people get to know each other and learn to accept differences. In a strong community, people do not feel judged and can be who they are even if that means they are far from perfect and do not always meet the group norms. Ideally, support is readily available in a community, and empathy, relationships and connections bind it and are inclusive of everyone.

Community can come in the form of family, neighbourhoods, schools, clubs, teams and cultural groups. In any such form, community is a strong contributing factor to wellbeing and resilience. A 40-year longitudinal study of 698 infants on the Hawaiian island of Kauai, which began in 1955, showed that strong bonds with a non-parent carer and connection to spiritual or community groups like the YMCA were protective factors in the development of resilience. The study found one-third of high-risk children displayed resilience despite highly problematic environmental and developmental background. The group who were resilient and went on to show growth and become caring and contributing members of the community as adults had strong connections to other people and the community outside of their family (Werner and Smith, 2001).

The complexities of modern family life, including divorce, separation and the creation of step-families, have had an impact on what community looks like. Families living in different areas of the country and overseas, away from grandparents and other extended family, have meant that these communities have had to adapt how they connect in new and more innovative ways.

Previous generations often lived in the same neighbourhood or even the same house, allowing stories to be handed down in a more fluid fashion. These stories can enrich family life and increase a sense of depth in a child's family history. They are also the basis for many of our developing values.

Lower wellbeing and mental resilience have been linked to isolation from family, friends and community (Werner and Smith, 2001). Having high levels of easily accessible support brings emotional strength and security. Having people around to laugh with and talk to is an extra source of wellbeing and joy, benefiting both young and old.

The place of schools in building community and connection

Schools provide an important opportunity to build a sense of community. Schools are by nature very social places. Learning doesn't happen in isolation; it happens in the context of others. When young people feel empathised with, and connected to their peers and broader school community, they are more likely to feel relaxed and resilient enough to handle the challenges of learning. They are more likely to behave according to the school values and to work harder on their performance (Zannetino, 2007).

A classroom where students mix with a variety of personalities and develop a range of relationships each year also provides good opportunities to build resilience. When relationships are strong, the commitment to maintain them is also strong and the students work hard to stay connected. While it can be counterproductive for certain students with strong personality clashes or high conflict to be placed together in the same class (particularly year after year), there is always an opportunity for social and emotional growth when students are expected to work closely with peers who are different from them. Students learn a lot and build resilience from challenges and exposure to imperfect circumstances. When class groups are devised to match personalities and learning needs precisely, opportunities to build skills around compromise, empathy, conflict resolution, problem solving and understanding are reduced. An attitude of guiding students to cope with their differences and build connections with a wide variety of personalities can be part of the class philosophy.

School communities can be built from a desire and commitment to grow connections and seek to understand each other. To build strong relationships and connections in a classroom or other group setting, this chapter aims to teach students to understand and accept each individual within the classroom. It provides opportunities for students to find out more about each other and learn from each other's differences. It also focuses on humility; teaching students to let their efforts, actions and achievements speak for themselves, to appreciate strengths in others and to avoid trying to always be better than everyone else.

Empathy

Providing young people with opportunities to learn about and practise empathy contributes to stronger communities. By nature, most people are programmed to empathise and feel concern for others when seeing them struggling and want to somehow help out (Goleman, 2006). Research into the brain's mirror neurons has been able to show that when someone watches someone feeling joy or pain, the same parts of the observer's brain are activated as those of the person who is actually experiencing the event (Gallese et al., 2005; Jacobini et al., 2005).

Explanation for young students

People usually like being around other people. Someone can be very shy and still be social, enjoying and needing other people's company. In strong friendships and communities people don't expect you to be perfect all the time (because nobody is perfect). In strong communities people listen, care, empathise, try to understand each other and work together as a team. They also forgive each other for their mistakes and focus on problem solving and seeking solutions to keep their friendships healthy and strong.

Community can happen in a family, a school, a neighbourhood, or in a group where people like doing things together. Relationships with others are always strongest when they understand each other's differences and where people can be honest and trustworthy.

Explanation for older students

Feeling connected to others is great for your sense of wellbeing and resilience. The more connections you have, the stronger you feel. Humans are social beings – they are programmed to seek out company and belonging to groups strengthens them. Being part of a bigger group of people, with whom you feel safe and comfortable, is often called a 'community'. This kind of community doesn't happen automatically or without effort. The world is full of challenges and differences between people. Learning to handle your own emotions, to empathise, to understand other people's feelings, and to appreciate differences is a great way to build friendships and a fulfilling sense of community.

Someone with empathy:

Lennon Maher

Lennon Maher, aged 7, raised over $5,000 for children around the world to own a bike, cutting down on their long walk to and from school each day.

When Lennon Maher was only 6 years old, he heard there are children in some countries who have to walk for hours to get to school each day. Lennon's **empathy** for the children who had to work so hard before even starting their school day kicked in and he came up with a plan. He asked his mum if it would be okay to walk to school once a week to raise money to buy as many bikes as possible to make things easier for them. Lennon's mum agreed to walk the 3.8 km home from school once a week. The walk took them between one and one and a half hours. They met many supporters in their **community** along the way and their **empathy** for his efforts meant the word spread fast. He registered a sponsorship page on ChildFund and raised over $5,000. At $99 a bike, that's a lot of children having an easier journey to school each day because of one boy's sense of **community** and **care**, which went far beyond his own community. Lennon's **empathy** gave him the motivation and energy to keep going, come rain, hail or shine. When asked about how he does it, Lennon says, 'Sometimes it's fun, sometimes it's hard yakka. We've done it in the sunshine and the rain.'

GROUP DISCUSSION AND BRAINSTORM: Feeling left out

Ask students to remember a time when they felt left out of a group, like they didn't belong. What did it feel like? What did you need at the time to cope? Did anyone give you what you needed? What got you out of that place? Do you know someone who is on the 'outer' now? What could you do if you knew someone on the 'outer'?

Developing a community statement to build relationships

Try creating a statement for your class or school that encourages better relationships and a sense of community. Guide your students to work in small groups or pairs. Meet as a group with a collection of ideas and aim to develop a statement that honours the different values nominated by your students.

An example of a community and relationship building statement is below. Remember when developing the statement that it does not need to be complicated or lengthy. The class could build on this further by creating a mural on a canvas (or school building) that represents the statement.

An example of a community statement to build relationships

We encourage (not undermine).

We work to be our best (not better than).

We measure ourselves against our own efforts (not against others).

We build (instead of destroying).

We understand and empathise (and do not judge).

'Empathy: how will you take action?' worksheet

Hand out the worksheet found at the end of this chapter to allow students to think about what empathy is and how they can use it every day to acknowledge and support the thoughts and feelings of those around them.

How do you feel when someone smiles at you?

A short conversation with your students . . .

Have you ever met a person who doesn't feel good when someone smiles at them? Smiling at another person can also feel good. When you smile your brain releases chemicals that make you feel happier and build your wellbeing. Even doing a pretend smile can trick your mind into feeling happier than you did before you smiled. In one study, researchers found that one smile can make you feel as good as 2,000 bars of chocolate or 16,000 pounds sterling! The same researchers found that smiling also lowers stress, makes your immune system stronger, and releases endorphins (your 'feel good' hormone).

Pass the smile

Challenge your students to smile at as many people as possible each day. Set a goal to be the smiliest class in the school. (This is great fun when every class in the school has the same goal – which they may or may not be aware of!) Challenge them to smile at every person they make eye contact with. At the end of the week ask students to share how they felt when they were smiling and being smiled at.

Hold the smile

For anywhere between an hour and a day, ask your students to try not to smile at each other (this is a classroom activity where everyone is aware of what is going on – not an activity for meal or play breaks where other students might get the wrong idea by the lack of smiling). Debrief afterwards about how not smiling affected their mood and how they might feel if they and others were like this for extended periods of time.

Connect-a-thon

Use the template provided for a connect-a-thon sponsorship found at the end of this chapter. This activity provides your students with motivation to collect as much money as possible for a charity while having the bonus of experiencing the joy of growing connections with others along the way.

The aim of the fundraiser is to be caught connecting with others and building relationships as much as possible over a one-week period. Each day there will be a half-hour to one-hour period where a teacher/parent/other trusted adult observes how much the student tries to connect and get along with people around them. Students will not know when that time is. At the end of each day teachers can award points to show how much students were seen connecting with others. Students can earn up to 20 points a day, with 5 points equalling an agreed amount of money. Students can ask parents and other people in their community to sponsor them and keep encouraging them to work hard to raise money for a charity they care deeply about.

Choose your reputation

A short conversation with your students . . .

What you say and do is for the most part heard or seen by someone else. Humans are social beings and your brain is designed to look for connections and friendships with other people. Whether you know it or not, you are quietly noticing everyone around you. When you see another person say or do something that makes you feel safe and good, you take notice and store away a positive thought about that person in your mind, and a connection begins. When you see another person say or do something that makes you feel uncomfortable, a connection is challenged. A 'reputation' is what people know you for and this comes from what they see you saying and doing. For example, if you are always the first to check on someone who is unhappy, you will build a reputation for being kind and caring. If you are often seen playing games according to the rules, you will build a reputation for being fair. If you often get into angry disagreements with others, you will build a reputation as a bully or fighter. Once people have seen you do something more than once they start to get an idea in their head about who they think you are. Once these ideas are in someone's mind they can be hard to change. It sometimes takes many more times doing the opposite of what your reputation is to make people change their mind about a label they have given you. The easiest thing to do is to be truthful, kind, fair and reasonable so the only reputation you can build is a good one.

Role plays: reputation

Divide the class into small groups to role play the following scenarios.

A group of people are sitting outside the school. They see a friend of theirs alone. When they look closer they see them holding a tiny bird that has fallen out of a tree. The friend is hand-feeding it with a pipette. Role play this and the conversation that the group have about the child caring for the bird.

A person in your class goes from one student to the next saying that other students don't like them. You start to work out that this person is trying to build their friendships by getting other people into arguments while they appear to be the peacekeeper. Role play this and the conversation that follows between group members about this person.

A person in your class often collects money for charity. They even had a birthday party and asked for no presents! Instead they asked for donations to their favourite charity. One day this person's family loses their house and all their belongings in a bushfire. Role play the conversation that follows your finding out the news, and make a plan about how you will help.

Every time the teacher starts to talk to the class someone makes silly noises and interrupts. This student does this in all classes and has been doing it for a long time. Role play a conversation teachers may have in the staff room about this student.

It's time to vote for the student representative council. Lots of people want to be voted in but there are only two places per class. Role play a group of students talking together about who they will vote for. Try and talk about as many different reputations as you can, explaining why you will or will not vote for someone.

Role plays: 'I understand' empathy

A note to the facilitator: Trying to understand another person's perspective when it is different from your own is one of the most valuable skills in connecting and building relationships. Too often when a difference occurs, the relationship is shut down in young minds that do not yet have the maturity to see things in perspective and to accept that friendships can continue even with differences of opinion. The following role plays provide students with an opportunity to try and decode behaviours that on the surface are upsetting but might not be as sinister underneath.

Someone in your group has become very quiet and doesn't want to chat much at play breaks. Try and come up with as many ideas as you can to understand what might be going on.

Your best friend is acting really bossy all of a sudden. They are always telling you what to do and it's driving you mad! Role play talking to a friend about what's going on as you try to understand the change in your best friend's behaviour.

Your teacher is grumpy today and whenever you ask for help they get cross with you. Role play talking to someone about it as you try and understand what's going on for your teacher.

A group of students in your class are really acting up. You find this behaviour very frustrating. The principal visited the class today and you were asked as the class representative to talk about the behaviour to help work out what is going on. Have a conversation with your principal where you try to help him or her understand why the group is acting up.

You're at sports practice and your friend hates to lose. Every time they come last they either say you cheated or make up some other excuse about why they didn't win. It is starting to spoil how you feel in sports practice. Role play talking to someone about it where you try to understand your friend's behaviour.

Your little brother is following you around more than usual. You really want some time alone and every time you ask your brother to leave he seems to follow you around even closer. You're starting to get really annoyed with him! Role play talking to someone about it where you try to understand your little brother's behaviour.

One world, so many ideas!

This exercise helps broaden student awareness about the richness of culture and variations in perspective. Choose a topic such as LOVE, FRIENDSHIP, WISDOM or HAPPINESS and provide a range of cultures to choose from. Each child pulls a culture from around the world out of a hat and researches how the culture interprets the topic. Challenge students to summarise this in fewer than five sentences and as close as possible to one sentence. Create a class poster, 'One world, so many ideas!' This activity can be repeated throughout the year for a number of topics.

Who's looking out for me?

Place students' names in a jar. At the beginning of each day or week ask each student to take a name out. For that day or week, it is their responsibility to look out for the student whose name they have drawn. They keep a special eye on them as if they were their guardian angel. At the end of the day or week, before leaving class, students reveal who they were keeping an eye on. It can also be fun to let everyone take one guess at who they think was looking out for them before the person is revealed. Some teachers have done this activity throughout the school year, where each week someone has somebody to focus on. Otherwise use it intermittently – particularly when class connectedness is disrupted.

Be my eyes and be my ears

This exercise in perspective taking is simple and easy. In pairs, students take it in turns to imagine what their partner could not hear but could see. The student then describes in detail the sounds around them. Next, the pairs swap and the other person imagines their partner cannot see but can hear and goes to much effort to describe what they can see (students can use a blindfold if they like for this part).

Community tubs

Provide each student with a medium-sized tub or container (ice-cream containers work well as do glass or plastic jars).

Explain to the students that they are decorating this container for someone special in their neighbourhood or community. While they decorate suggest they think about the people around them who make them feel supported and encouraged, or perhaps they can think of a person who is alone or having a difficult time.

At this stage do not tell the students the purpose of the activity. Once the containers are decorated, ask each student to write the name of the person they were thinking of on the lid. Now explain the tubs are to be filled with something hand-made, hand-picked or hand-written. Some children might like to bring something from home and others might need your help to fill the tub.

A note for parents about the activity is found at the end of this paragraph to explain the purpose of the activity. When the tubs are delivered it is best done in person rather than leaving it on a doorstep. Attach a card to the person explaining why they have been chosen to receive the tub and that, if they wish, they can re-use the tub to fill for a person they feel connected to in their community.

Dear Parent/Guardian/Carer,

Our class is exploring what it means to be part of a community and the importance of empathising with others. Your child has chosen someone they know who they feel is either very supportive of them or needs support because of a challenge. Please help your child fill their container with something home-made or grown that you are happy to share. Your child will need your help to deliver it as well. If you have any difficulties please let me know so I can help.

With thanks,

Individual contribution: sharing roles and responsibilities amongst the class

Within the classroom and school there are usually many opportunities for age-appropriate contribution. Finding ways for your students to contribute to benefit your classroom or school provides them with confidence and a sense that their contribution is making a difference to their school. It also alleviates work for the teacher. Students can rotate jobs on a roster, as shown below.

- Greeter (person who goes to anyone who knocks on the door or enters the classroom unexpectedly during learning time)
- Materials manager (checks on stationery supplies etc. at the end of each week and replenishes as needed)
- Computer technician
- Bookshelf monitor
- Meeting chairperson
- Inspiration manager (responsible for writing something inspiring at the start of each day on the board)
- Kindness detective (person who keeps their eyes and ears out for acts of kindness and good will in the classroom)
- Plant/garden maintenance team
- Phone manager
- Diary monitor
- Book coverer
- Peer support leader
- Laminating assistant
- Class manager
- Window cleaner
- Pet monitor
- Interior decorating advisors
- Class counsellors (available to listen (not advise) when someone is having a difficult time)
- Teacher's personal assistant
- Smiler (someone whose goal it is to smile as much as possible to get the whole class smiling too!)
- Relaxation enthusiast (someone who makes sure the stress levels of students are being recognised and responded to)

Make sure you alternate responsibilities frequently (weekly to fortnightly) so that students stop a responsibility while they are still enjoying it. This works even better if students are part of the original discussion about what jobs are needed in a classroom to keep it running smoothly, and students suggest how they can help their teachers. You might also like to suggest class rewards such as outdoor play, free time, or watching a movie when the class have been carrying out their jobs so well that you feel you have much more time on your hands.

For health professionals working with young people outside the school setting you might like to look into ways to contribute to a charity or a community project.

School volunteer network

Consider starting up a volunteer network within the school. Provide a display board for students to post areas where they are happy to help other students (sports, learning, friendship, homework, goal setting and so forth). On the other side of the board students can post a comment when they feel they need help with something at school. You can frequently check the board to maintain awareness about where some students are struggling and also seek to match a volunteer with a student in need. Where possible set up opportunities for the help to be accessed; and make sure to gain parental consent before a child adds volunteering to their existing routines.

Class encouragement pigeon holes

Provide your class with mailboxes/in-trays/pigeon holes where notes of encouragement and kindness can gather. Allow time every day or every week where students can take time to think about someone in their class who is working hard and could do with encouragement, or someone in their class who deserves kind words. Students place these notes into their peers' pigeon holes. Remind students not to keep placing notes in the same person's pigeon hole. Students are welcome to place notes at other times as well. In some classes where dynamics have been challenging, it can be useful to have a class discussion beforehand about why it is important that all notes are positive and encouraging, and what the consequences should be if someone breaks that value.

Cake bake off roster

Create a school roster that only teachers can access to allow for the element of surprise. On any given day, a class on the cake roster will be provided with all the ingredients necessary to bake a large cake (or several cupcakes) for another class. (Make sure allergies are considered in your planning. Avoid nuts in *all* cases.) If you are able to access large baking trays this will be particularly useful. Bake together and enjoy the flow of cooking. Once you have made plenty of cakes, allow a small group of students to surprise another class with their produce. Students will feel pride as they generously share their efforts, and the recipients will delight in the freshly baked cake! When this is done as a whole school activity it creates quite a buzz amongst students who wonder when it will be their turn to bake (and of course receive!)

Well wishing

Teach your students the gentle art of wishing those around them well. With competition in the classroom, yard and in sports many children feel they have to work hard to be the best. When others do better than them their jealousy can overwhelm them. The idea of wishing others well in their pursuits places student minds in a positive frame of reference and, with practice, well wishing can become enjoyable and make coming second or even last much easier.

A well wish doesn't need to be said aloud (but can be). It is about taking a moment in the mind to say, 'good luck', 'be happy', 'have fun', 'go for it', 'I hope your hard work pays off'. You can extend this further by suggesting students wish others well who are suffering in some way. If they see someone is sick they can wish for them to get better. If they see someone is lonely, they can wish them company, or better, provide them with company! Encouraging your students to try and look beyond their own experiences and be in tune with those around them keeps them connected to others and focused on their values.

Balloon in a box

Hand out a balloon to each student with a marker that is easy to use on the rubber. Allow some time to think of positive statements they can write on them. Then tie a small card to each balloon saying, 'You have received a smile from a stranger! Blow and enjoy!' Take your class for a walk in the schoolyard or locker area. One by one the balloons are dropped in people's bags. This random act of kindness is fun and exciting to do and children often reflect for some time on who might have blown up their balloon and what their response might have been!

We can work this out together

Divide the class into pairs or small groups (pairs is ideal for younger students). Hand each pair or group a ball/other sports equipment and assign them the job of inventing a game, complete with rules, where they are competing against each other. Encourage them to work out how they will handle disputes and watch them build their relationship through this challenge. Be available to help as much as possible. This creates an opportunity to self-regulate and stay connected in order to share some fun with another person.

Sandstone sculptures

This activity is a playful way to practise intuition and connection with others while tapping into their creativity. Divide the class into pairs and hand each child a piece of sandstone (this is easy to sculpt and available in most art and craft stores). Another option is to use bars of soap, plasticine or clay. Ask students to think about their partner and to imagine what they might like sculpted. Allow the pair to sit together for five minutes during which they try and pass each other a mental message about what they would like sculpted for them. A broad theme is optional. If you are using a theme, some suggestions are:

Vehicles, animals, insects, one of the Seven Wonders of the World, a famous landmark, summer, sea animals, household items.

Provide the students with a space to sit apart from each other for sculpting. At the end of the activity they present their partner with their sculpture and give it as a gift. Watch the connections and fun they have giving and receiving.

Teacher and student bonding: student–teacher interviews

The relationship between a student and their teacher is one of the most influential aspects of student learning and engagement (Liberante, 2012). When a student feels connected to their teacher, a unique trust and confidence develops. When that connection is particularly strong, part of the student's learning and behaviour motivation comes from wanting to stay connected to their teacher by behaving respectfully and fulfilling learning responsibilities to the best of their efforts. Teachers also have the role of disciplinarian, guiding positive behaviour and effort. When this is done with kindness and understanding, students thrive. Some students take longer to form connections with. The following ideas can help forge this connection.

Take an individual student to your desk and allow some time to conduct a get-to-know-you interview based either on the following questions or ones you have chosen:

What is your favourite holiday celebration and why?
If you could visit any country in the world where would it be and why?
If you could change one thing about school what would it be?
Do you collect anything or have any hobbies?

Teacher reports

Not all teachers feel comfortable doing this activity and it is by no means essential to relationship building. If you feel this would work in your class, let your students know early on in the year that at the end of each term they are allowed to write a report on you.

Hand out the teacher report found at the end of this chapter and see what comes of it! When you allow this amount of transparency as a teacher it can do wonders for your connections with your students. Even better, if a student gives you a low mark in something, take it seriously and let them explain it to you personally. Another way to encourage feedback is to have a 'compliments and complaints' box on your desk for students to communicate with you. This is not suitable for all classes but when it works it can be a lot of fun!

Student and teacher share a memory

Find time at the end of each term to ask each student what their favourite memory of the term is, but it must be about a moment you shared together. You can then share your favourite memory of the term about the student you are talking to.

Me three

Students are asked to choose up to three items from home that reflect something about themselves. They should be prepared to share these items with their class or in small groups. Encourage students to choose items revealing something other students are unlikely to know about them. Sharing these items opens up a space for empathy, understanding and relationship development where students see another side to their peers.

Me in here

Allow students a couple of minutes to look around the classroom. Either in groups or as a class, ask each student to choose something in the room that represents some aspect of themselves. For example, a person might choose a pencil because they love to draw. Another person might choose an eraser because they are good at forgiving others. The class must try and guess why each person has chosen a particular item.

Peer mentoring

This activity can be as short as one week or as long as one year. In fact some teachers have tried to maintain peer mentoring relationships between students over several years. Work with another teacher in your school with students two or more years above or below your students. It can also be done with students in the same year level – particularly if the mentoring is around learning.

Pair each child with one from another class and explain their role as mentors to each other. This is a two-sided relationship and the younger student is also asked to see himself or herself as a mentor, even though the other student is older. The pairs meet in a structured way at least once a month but are also asked to maintain the relationship by looking out for each other in the yard and doing what they can to be an inspiration to the other by living each day with authenticity and care. This is a wonderful way to extend a sense of community throughout a school while increasing learning outcomes (Hattie, 2008).

Bullying role plays: a note to facilitators

Bullying comes in many forms. Sometimes it is verbal, other times physical. There is 'overt' bullying where the bully openly targets others, and 'covert' bullying where the bully skilfully harasses out of sight and earshot of others. Sometimes the bully makes the problem look like it lies in the other person. No matter how the bullying appears, it is important to take a strong and consistent stand against it. Bullying has the potential to damage the spirit and impact on the victim's ability to learn and feel connected. Multiple relationships can be affected and one bully in any type of community can do a significant amount of damage.

At the start of the school year, teachers can lay down boundaries about what behaviour they will and won't accept. They can identify what bullying looks like and the importance of exposing it no matter what the bully threatens. Make it clear your class values are anti-bullying and focus on kindness, encouragement, growth and relationships.

The following role plays will open up discussions around the importance of saying 'no' to bullying, so that relationships can thrive and the class and school community can stay strong and connected.

Divide the class into pairs or small groups and ask them to perform the following role plays with a solution.

You save money each week to spend in the tuck shop. For the last few weeks someone has been asking you to buy them food using your money. The first time you got them something but you are now feeling frustrated and know you have the right to say 'no' to this.

One of your classmates insists you do everything with them. As soon as it is time to work in pairs or go out to play, they grab your arm. You would really like to pair up with some of your other friends, but when you try, they get really sad and say, 'you hate me don't you?'

Someone in the year above you calls you horrible names at playtime. They say things that really embarrass and hurt you. You are starting to feel sick at the thought of playtime, which used to be your favourite part of the day.

You have had some trouble learning some new concepts in maths. Whenever you put your hand up and ask a question a group of other students either repeat your question in a silly voice or laugh at you. You find it hard enough as it is, asking for help, but now you're feeling like you would be better off falling behind and not asking questions than being laughed at and mocked by these students.

Someone new at your school is getting bullied every day by a student in your class. No one is doing anything about it but it is really upsetting you. You are waiting to buy something from the tuck shop when you see the bully take the new person's tuck shop money.

There's a person in your class who chooses different people to 'leave out' of games and conversations each day. Sometimes you are the one and other times it's your friends. When it happens to your friends you feel too scared to speak up because you know it will probably be you next time. You want it to stop.

Whenever you play sport at lunchtime your friends tell you you're really bad at the game. You love playing sport but you are feeling so upset by their comments you are thinking of doing something else at lunchtime.

Your friend has never given you a compliment before. When you do well in something they change the subject to something about themselves. Your friend is also very good at pointing out your weaknesses and challenges. Even when you are not so worried about them, they talk about it so much you do start to worry! You actually like being around this person most of the time but the bullying makes you feel unhappy.

Building community

Getting involved with the local council

Local councils often have many initiatives that allow schools and communities to get involved in planning and recreation in the local area. Teaching your students about the local council and its responsibilities, as well as grabbing opportunities as they arise to get your students involved in council activities, increases the sense of community as well as helping them build relationships outside of their immediate community. Some local councils fund small projects as well. Your students could work on ideas that would benefit their area and apply for small grants together.

Community gardens

More and more areas are appearing with community gardens. The idea is that people who do not have a garden can still benefit from the joys of gardening by accessing a small plot to grow plants and vegetables. These are a great place to visit for inspiration – particularly on an open day when the students can experience first-hand the sense of community that builds within the group who garden together. Bring the inspiration back to school and start a kitchen garden or other planting project.

Take a neighbourhood walk

Take your students for regular walks around the neighbourhood to broaden their sense of community around their school. Taking local walks like these helps children build their community identity. It is always exciting when students can point out their homes or favourite places along the way, deepening the sense of belonging. You can set projects for older students where they identify the nature of the neighbourhood and what makes it different from other neighbourhoods, what the local landmarks are, who lives around the neighbourhood and so on.

Visit local nursing homes

Local nursing homes are often happy to schedule visits from students to present a performance or spend time getting to know the residents. There is so much value for young people in meeting people outside of their generation and hearing their stories. Starting up as pen pals then meeting can be a wonderful opportunity to build new relationships for your students as well as increase their sense of community.

Encourage your students to build friendships outside of school: journal entry

Making friends outside of school and family groups helps build individual identity and confidence. Ask your students what it might mean if you only had friends at school. What might be the advantages? What might be the disadvantages? Students can take out their journals and write down names of friends that do not go to their school. Cousins are often very special to children so certainly allow them to include extended family in this list. The main objective is to help students understand that if they have a variety of friendships they will usually have someone or somewhere to fall back on when things become difficult in one environment. In other words they do not have all their eggs in one basket.

Weekly challenge to further develop the skill

Think of someone in your class you have trouble getting along with. It might be someone who keeps to themselves, has strong opinions different from yours, or even someone who bullies you. Spend the week trying to see the world through their eyes. Try understanding where your differences come from and what emotions your differences trigger in you. If you feel comfortable, try extending yourself to get to know them better. Smile at them, talk to them, and compliment them. See if you can build a connection with them even though you feel disconnected from them.

Parent tips

Model and encourage good relationships

Your children learn a lot from watching. Some of their favourite people to watch are parents of course. Most children grow up wanting to be like mum and dad. Show them you focus on kindness, understanding and encouragement in all your relationships. Show them you handle conflict respectfully. Listen. Show thanks and appreciation often. Avoid gossiping around your children and never make them feel they have to take

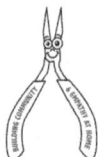

sides if you are having conflict with someone else they love. Keep information about adult conflicts to the bare minimum. Be the person you want your child to be! When they have a conflict with a friend, help them work it out using the skills you have been modelling.

Make relationships the number one focus

While your job as a parent is to guide and direct your child, it is helpful to develop a loving and understanding relationship with them where they can experience unconditional love. Children grow when they know they are loved for who they are and not for who their parents want them to be. When your child needs guidance and discipline, try doing it in a way where they can learn something without feeling criticised or misunderstood. By listening, empathising and seeking to understand your child, you are building your relationship to last a lifetime.

Make boundaries against bullying between siblings clear in your home

Most siblings argue daily over small things as they learn to share, handle different opinions and negotiate play. The arguments change as siblings grow older and they become more about respecting privacy and personality differences. These are all normal and healthy ways to build relationship skills and handle strong emotions in a safe and loving environment. Bullying each other crosses an acceptable boundary in any relationship and it should be no different in the sibling relationship. Two children fighting over the remote control or about who can run the fastest can usually be managed without adult intervention. Put downs and set ups on the other hand fall easily into the bullying category and a firm and consistent stand should be taken, with a clear message, 'We encourage in this family. We do not bully or set people up to get into trouble.' Stay confident and the message stays clear. They will get used to it soon enough.

Teach your children how to handle conflict well

We teach our children so many new things from the moment they are born. If you teach children how to manage conflict well, it is a skill they will use throughout their lives. Conflict is inevitable at home, at school, in sport, and later on in the workplace. Sometimes it is big, usually it is small, but conflict handled badly can make mountains out of molehills. Teach your child to remember there are two sides to every argument – otherwise it wouldn't be an argument! Both people think their ideas are just as right and important. Restorative practices allow children to consider other people's thoughts, feelings and perspectives. This approach does not look at who started it or who is to blame, it simply looks at a resolution and seeks to repair the relationship. When conflict is solved restoratively, children do not think you are taking sides (and hence loving the other sibling more) and maintain their relationship despite their differences.

Listen well

Children talk a lot! There is nothing more frustrating to them when they are telling you a story about something and they can tell you're not listening. Because it is impossible to listen all the time, it is better to tell your child, 'I can't listen right now', or, 'I really want to hear about this after I finish this job', rather than to pretend you're listening and get caught red-handed being distracted. Then, when you are listening, you can be a great role model for listening. Maintain eye contact, nod, smile and encourage them to keep talking. Show empathy when they share their feelings, and enjoy this wonderful exchange. One quality conversation like this is worth much more than a multitude of scattered and distracted chats.

Put mobile devices away when it is focused family time

That beep of a message or email coming through on your phone is designed to grab your attention. Our love of human connection makes us want to check it straight away to see who it's from and what they are saying. The thing is, when we do this around others we are treating our phones like another person and interrupting real time relationships for something else. We are role modelling that the phones are really important. Even if you choose one hour a day where you put your phone on silent or keep it away from you, then you allow yourself to indulge in quality time without distraction. This is so good for relationship building. It might even mean when your child is a teenager they won't be glued to their device when you're spending time together.

Encourage neighbourhood play

Seeing children play without structure and without parents in their neighbour-hood does not have to be a thing of the past. By working together with your neighbours or allowing yourself to be there to supervise but not so close your child can still converse with you, your children can enjoy the benefits of neighbourhood play and the friendships that can evolve. Whether on bikes, on foot, on scooters, or playing sports, this kind of free play really is bliss. Once children are responsible enough to play like this, they can be the judge of what is and isn't safe. They will tune into their own instincts instead of relying on a closely observing parent. They will be able to leave an interaction when they feel they have had enough time socialising rather than when the play date officially ends. They will develop skills about relationships and tune in to their own understanding about which friends are positive to spend time with and which ones are not. The sense of community and connection this can bring to children and adults alike is immeasurable.

Broaden their friendship circle

All families struggle from time to time with the inevitable juggle of their children's school, sports, hobbies, projects and parties. With each extra child in the family comes more juggling. While it is clear how important it is not to commit children to too many things, one or two activities outside of school can be really beneficial. Children build resilience through relationships and a sense that they have a group of people who care for them. The more connections we have outside our family, the stronger we feel. When children are able to build relationships outside of school with friends extending into the neighbourhood and beyond, they will always have people and places to fall back on when faced with social challenges and they will not feel like all their eggs are in one basket.

Get involved in your local community

Even if it's just using local parks or taking neighbourhood walks, chatting to neighbours along the way, these interactions are showing your children how important the community around you is. If you have time to volunteer at park upgrades, planting and other local events, get your children involved too, and enjoy the sense of community it builds.

Respond to a local council survey about what you feel would be great for your neighbourhood

Local councils often invite public opinion about new parks and projects, asking what people in the neighbourhood would like to see improved. Rather than popping these surveys straight into the recycling or 'too hard' basket, find a moment to sit with your children and help them write a response. Show them their opinion in the community is important. While not all of their ideas will come to fruition, chances are from time to time they will see something and remember they were part of that project and that some of their ideas were included in the final product.

EMPATHY:
HOW WILL YOU TAKE ACTION?

When someone around you is having a difficult time, try and take action. Showing empathy means you take time to care and try to understand what the other person is thinking and feeling. Draw a picture or write down what you could do to show empathy in the following situations.

Empathy Needed Please	Take Action By...
1. Someone has fallen down in front of their sports team. They are crying and no one is helping.	
2. Someone in the class has just got into trouble and everyone in the class is mad at them because now, everyone has to stay in.	
3. Someone in your class doesn't understand the work but is too shy to ask the teacher for help. You notice them quietly crying at their desk.	
4. You have just been invited to a birthday party and you are so excited. You see someone in your class who hardly ever gets invited to anything looking lonely. They were one of the only people in the class to not get an invitation.	
5. You see someone from your class alone in the yard. You don't really enjoy playing with them and neither do most of your friends.	

CONNECT-A-THON: WATCH ME CONNECT WITH OTHERS

Monday	Tuesday	Wednesday	Thursday	Friday	Saturday	Sunday
$	$	$	$	$	$	$

TEACHER REPORT

Give your teacher fair and constructive marks out of ten for their teaching. Take the questions seriously and respectfully. If you think your teacher can improve in a certain area be respectful about how you explain it to them.

TEACHER'S NAME:

STUDENT'S NAME:

DATE:

Ratings are out of ten (please circle). Ten = couldn't do better. Five = pretty good. 1 = I wish there was more of this.

FUN	1	2	3	4	5	6	7	8	9	10
VARIETY	1	2	3	4	5	6	7	8	9	10
INSPIRATION	1	2	3	4	5	6	7	8	9	10
EXPLAINING THINGS	1	2	3	4	5	6	7	8	9	10
KEEPING US ACTIVE	1	2	3	4	5	6	7	8	9	10
UNDERSTANDING	1	2	3	4	5	6	7	8	9	10

COMMENTS (write a short comment about your teacher here)

KINDNESS RECORD SHEET

"When given the choice between being right and being kind, choose kind" (Wayne Dyer)
When you do something kind, write and draw about it here. Aim to do three kind things every day!

1._____
_____
_____
_____

2._____
_____
_____
_____

3._____
_____
_____
_____

4._____
_____
_____
_____

5._____
_____
_____
_____

6._____
_____
_____
_____

7._____
_____
_____
_____

1.

2.

3.

4.

5.

6.

7.

Reference list

Diener, E. and Seligman, M. E. P. 2004. 'Beyond Money: Toward an Economy of Well-Being'. *Psychological Science in the Public Interest* Vol. 5 No. 1, pp. 1–31.

Gallese, V. et al. 2005. 'Intentional Attunement: Mirror Neurones and the Neural Underpinnings of Interpersonal Relationships'. University of Padua, Italy.

Goleman, D. 2006. *Social Intelligence: The New Science of Social Relationships*. New York: Bantam Books.

Hattie, J. 2008. *Visible Learning for Teachers: Maximizing Impact on Learning*. London: Routledge.

Jacobini, M. et al. 2005. 'Grasping the Intentions of Others with One's Own Mirror Neuron System'. *PLOS Biology* Vol. 5, pp. 29–35.

Liberante, L. 2012. 'The Importance of Teacher-Student Relationships, as Explored Through the Lens of the NSW Quality Teaching Model'. *Journal of Student Engagement: Education Matters* Vol. 2 No. 1, pp. 2–9 (University of Woollongong, Australia).

Werner, E. and Smith, S. 2001. *Journeys from Childhood to Midlife: Risk Resilience and Recovery*. Ithaca, NY: Cornell University Press.

Zannetino, L. 2007. 'Belonging, Connectedness, and Self-Worth: Building Socially Sustainable Communities through a School-Based Student Support Program'. *Journal of Student Well-Being* Vol. 1 No. 1, pp. 1–14 (University of South Australia, Adelaide).

4 Problem solving

We cannot solve our problems with the same thinking we used when we created them.

Albert Einstein

Introduction for teachers and health professionals

Whether it's working out what to do when you've left your lunch money at home or figuring out how to deal with bullies, carefully crafted problem solving lies at the heart of a good solution. Knowing how to deal with problems, big or small, builds resilience (Pearson and Kordich Hall, 2008). It feels good to know what to do when things don't go as planned and it's much easier to bounce back from adversity when you anticipate a solution.

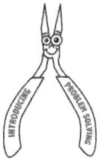

Many young people feel overwhelmed when they're faced with a problem. In a world of high and often unrealistic standards and expectations around happiness, the word 'problem' itself is enough to make them feel like something is wrong with them if they experience one. Yet, who doesn't have problems to deal with? Add those who've grown up with adults around them taking on their problems for them without allowing them to rise to their own challenges and you have a young person without the confidence to solve their own problems. When everyday squabbles with peers and siblings, challenges with organisation, making decisions and so forth are handled and resolved by adults, young children grow into older people who continue to rely on others to solve their problems. Feeling like you can't handle life's challenges and needing to be rescued is a sure way to lower your resilience and wellbeing.

In *The Optimistic Child*, Seligman (2007) points out how rescuing children from their problems by trying to 'fix' them for them will give them a message of 'you can't handle this on your own' (p. 237). Showing you care and are prepared to offer guidance can be done without offering solutions or dictating what to do, by encouraging the development of independent problem solving skills.

The framework offered in this chapter is useful for all young people to use to problem solve. Younger students will need to see problem solving modelled and will need assistance to do so most of the time as emotions for them are often the driving force for their actions. This chapter also reminds students that some problems need compromise in order to find a solution. When children are able to compromise they develop better empathy, perspective and become more flexible thinkers. Being able to compromise increases resilience as setbacks aren't globalised or seen as fixed. It is also great for everyone's wellbeing as it shifts the energy invested in power struggles towards solutions.

Explanation for older children

Problems are part of life. Nothing goes to plan all the time. Some problems are small and pass so quickly you hardly notice them – like not knowing where you left your school diary and having to trace your steps back until you work out where you left it. Other problems are bigger, like having trouble with your school work or knowing how to handle a person who is being mean to you. These challenges tend to hang around for a while until you work on a plan to solve them.

Problems are challenges – obstacles – puzzles. They exercise your brain and make you smarter (if you plan to solve them that is!). You can either get caught up in the frustration of a problem and put all your energy into that, or you can accept problems happen and focus on what it takes to solve them.

By deciding to be a problem solver you give your brain the chance to practise new skills that build a better brain. You also build your wellbeing and resilience as you prove to yourself you can handle anything when you're willing to put the time and effort into finding solutions.

Explanation for younger children

Problem is the word for when something doesn't happen the way you wanted it to. You might feel sad, frustrated, annoyed or worried. Some problems are small, like a friend being away sick and you missing them at playtime. Problems like this don't usually happen over and over again. Some problems are more upsetting, like leaving your lunch at home and you being hungry! Bigger problems might be handling bullies or not understanding the school work.

Being a problem solver means you make a plan to work things out. Problem solving makes your brain strong. It grows millions of new connections the more you work things out for yourself. Most of the time you are the best person to solve your problems. When you feel you are not safe or can't think of a solution no matter how hard you have tried, then ask for help.

Someone who problem solved:

Evans Wadongo

Evans was 19 when he developed the first African-designed and -produced solar lamp. One of CNN's Top Ten Heroes, the Schwab Foundation named him Social Entrepreneur of the Year, while *Esquire* magazine had him on their list of '20 Men Who Will Shape the Next 20 Years'.

Evans called his solar-powered lamps 'MwangaBora', which means 'good light' when translated from Swahili. Evans knew most children in his hometown near Nairobi couldn't study at night because they had no access to electricity. This was a **problem** that bothered him a lot. He wanted to find a **solution** and worked hard at school, enduring a 10-kilometre walk to and from school every day. Evans finished school in the top 100 students of Kenya.

As a young engineer, he was 19 when his **problem solving** led to a **solution**. He invented the first lamp in Africa powered by the sun. This eliminated the need to buy kerosene (which has harmful side effects, is a fire risk and pollutes the air through its emissions). Evans travelled to Malawi to launch the @sdfakenya partnership with the Jacaranda Foundation, training orphans to make solar lamps. The solar lamps were designed in a way that was so easy to replicate that young people could produce them on their own and make a living out of it. Forbes named him among '30 under 30' – of Africa's best young entrepreneurs – and he became a finalist for the Humanitarian Hero Award. He also received the Pan Commonwealth Youth Award and the African International Achievers Award.

'Be the boss of problem solving' (BOSS): guide sheet

Hand out the guide sheet found at the end of the chapter to show students useful steps to solve a problem.

Solving problems: plus and minus solutions worksheet

Hand out the worksheet found at the end of this chapter to help students practise noticing the advantages and disadvantages of various solutions. This worksheet can be used any time a student is having trouble making a decision or solving a problem.

Role plays: problem solving

Working in pairs, students can use the problem solving guide sheet and plus and minus worksheet as a framework for finding solutions to the following problems. Ask your students to pace themselves and demonstrate their understanding of the information they have learnt by showing it in the role play and where appropriate talking their thoughts through out loud.

Role plays for younger students

> You have left your school lunch at home. You are hungry. What are two plans you can try?

> Your mum is not there at school pick-up time. Other mums and dads are gone and you are still waiting. What are two plans you could try?

> You don't understand what the teacher just taught the class. Everyone else is working and you don't know what to do. What are two plans you can try?

> Your best friend is away sick and it's lunch play. You don't know who to play with. What are two plans you can try?

> Someone is being mean to you every break time and lunch. What are two plans you can try?

> You really want to play soccer with your friends at lunchtime but you are having trouble keeping up with them and joining in. They are fast and they have been playing a lot longer than you!

Role plays for older students

You want to join scouts with your friends but you already do drama and soccer. Your parents' rule is 'no more than two out-of-school activities'. What are two plans you could try?

Someone who used to be your friend has started bullying you. They've told you if you tell anyone about what's going on they will make everyone at school hate you. What are two plans you can try?

You walked to school this morning and realise it is casual day. You are the only person in a school uniform. You are embarrassed. You do not have keys to your house and your parents have left for work. What are two plans you could try?

You discover an unkind note written by two of your friends about another friend. What are two plans you could try?

You feel really stressed. You don't feel like you can keep up with your school work and in a couple of subjects you are far behind. What are two plans you could try?

You do better than expected in a maths test. You usually struggle with maths and failed your last test. You worked hard to prepare for this test and had help to prepare from a tutor. A rumour starts among other students that you cheated. You didn't cheat. What are two plans you could try?

Practice activities using the problem solving framework 'BOSS'

1 Breathing

Learning to slow your breathing to calm yourself down and think more clearly is the first step in being a good problem solver. There are lots of different breathing techniques out there to try. This one is called 4 – 7 – 8 and it's really easy and it works! Here's how:

Breathe in slowly to the count of 4 seconds . . . hold your breath for 7 seconds . . . breathe out slowly (through tight pursed lips) for 8 seconds. Take a few regular slow breaths in between and repeat 4 – 7 – 8 at least five times. To get really good at this you can practise it every day for five minutes. All breathing techniques work best when you have practised them many times. It isn't very helpful to just use the breathing when you are upset. It is hard to do something you haven't practised when you're upset.

2 Observe

Show your students a short TV show or excerpt from a TV show. Older students will enjoy *Fawlty Towers*, *Third Rock from the Sun*, *Mr Bean*, *The Big Bang Theory* and so on. Younger students will be able to put their observation skills to work from watching *Charlie and Lola*, *Peppa Pig*, *Mr Bean*, *Humf* and so on. At the point where the problem in the story occurs, pause the DVD and ask students how important observation and listening are when you are with other people. Offer the following questions:

What's the problem?
Who is most upset about the problem?
What are the other characters thinking and feeling?
What else is going on around the problem?
What might be possible solutions to the problem?

Now return to the show and enjoy watching your students watch what happens next.

3 Set goals

To practise step 3, offer problems from the list below. Challenge your students to work in small groups and come up with at least three potential goals from the same problem. The goal is simply what they want to happen next. Discuss how different people will have different goals for the same problem. The goal they come up with might not be something they would do themselves. The challenge is to try and think like another person might.

Role plays for younger students

Your parents have just told you off for something your brother did. What is your goal – what do you want to happen?

You forgot it was your turn for show and share today. You don't have anything to show your class. What is your goal – what do you want to happen?

You bullied someone at break time and you feel bad about it. What is your goal – what do you want to happen?

You took something belonging to one of your friends without asking and you feel bad. What is your goal – what do you want to happen?

You lost your friend's football cards and she is asking where they are. What is your goal – what do you want to happen?

You don't understand the maths challenge your teacher has just set. What is your goal – what do you want to happen?

Role plays for older students

> You saw someone being bullied. What is your goal – what do you want to happen?

> You are given detention for something you didn't do. What is your goal – what do you want to happen?

> You left your mouth guard at home and it is sports practice. What is your goal – what do you want to happen?

> You are way behind on a school project. What is your goal – what do you want to happen?

> You found some money in the schoolyard. What is your goal – what do you want to happen?

> You bullied someone. What is your goal – what do you want to happen?

> You said something mean about a friend to someone and your friend is asking you about it. What is your goal – what do you want to happen?

4 Seek solutions – add pluses and minuses

Use the problems in the goal setting activity above to come up with four solutions complete with pluses and minuses for the problem. Journal the answer or role play in pairs.

Sample solutions to solve a problem

- Walk away
- Use relaxation and breathing
- Learn new skills
- Practise skills
- Ask for help
- Decide to 'let it go' and take your focus off it
- Write in a journal about the problem
- Talk to someone about your feelings
- Compromise
- Be active
- Talk to the person you are having the problem with
- Write your feelings down in a journal
- Get busy doing things that bring you pleasure
- Role play talking to the person involved in the problem
- Goal set

BRAINSTORM: Check back – what was I thinking?

Remind students it's good to check back on a solution you used to work through a problem. We learn from mistakes and mastery. Remembering to check back is not always easy. Open a brainstorm about how students could make sure they do check back on their plans following a problem.

Why is it important to check your ideas or solutions worked or didn't work?
How might someone remember to do this?
What might get in the way of someone remembering to check back on his or her solutions?

Compromise in problem solving

A short conversation with your students . . .

A lot of problems are actually disagreements between two or more people wanting different things. In the schoolyard the problem needing compromise might be two friends who can't agree on what to play. In the classroom, the problem needing comprise might be your teacher wanting you to pack up an activity and you wanting to continue with it. At home, the problem needing compromise might be mum or dad wanting you to go to bed at a certain time and you thinking you should be allowed to stay up later.

A compromise is roughly the halfway point between two different wishes. Compromises are not suitable when safety is at risk, the law opposes it, or when a wish crosses other people's personal boundaries.

COMPROMISE MEANS GIVING UP A BIT OF WHAT YOU WANT AND TAKING ON A BIT OF WHAT THE OTHER PERSON WANTS. ANOTHER WAY TO PUT IT IS, 'MEET HALFWAY.'

Compromise journal entry

You can cut the individual problems out and hand them to students, or record them on the whiteboard.

Allow students to consider the problems below, and to record the opposing wishes needing compromise in their journals. This activity can also be done as a brainstorm – particularly for young people. Simply ask, 'what do the two people want?'

Problem 1: One skipping rope is left and two children are looking at it.

Problem 2: One child wants to play soccer and the other child wants to play something else.

Problem 3: Mum says no to a treat before dinner and the child is holding tight to the chocolate bar they just found.

Problem 4: A child wants to walk to school alone and their parents say, 'no'.

Problem 5: The parents want a big vegetable patch but the children want a larger play area.

Problem 6: A group is planning a project together and can't agree on one idea.

Problem 7: One child in the family wants a pet cat and the other is scared of cats.

Problem 8: The family plan to go on a holiday. The children want to go to the beach and the parents want to go to the countryside.

Problem 9: A child wants to stay up later and their parents want their bedtime to stay the same.

Problem 10: A child wants a birthday party every year and their parents want one every two years.

Problem 11: A child wants to go bushwalking but is refusing to wear suitable clothes to protect them from the weather and snakes.

Problem 12: The family want to watch a movie together but every movie night there's an argument between the children about what to watch.

Problem 13: Each child in the family wants special time alone with one of the parents on the weekend. The family is busy and it is hard to fit in special alone time for one child.

A final word on compromise: a note to the facilitator

Compromise is not easy. Plenty of adults struggle with it. To be able to compromise there needs to be an open and empathetic conversation. It always works best if the adult lets the child go first and asks, 'What do you want?', showing they understand by reflecting the information back. The adult then states, 'What I would like is . . .', and together they work out a rough halfway point where both parties get a little of what they want. This is much better than all or nothing. It is good for the relationship too – it models flexibility and empathy. Once you reach an agreement, it helps to shake hands on it and where appropriate create a brief visual contract that solidifies your agreement.

Problem solving through disagreements

Offer students the guide at the end of the chapter to look at how to solve a problem with a friend. Teaching young people to resolve conflict in a fair and empathetic way, focusing on repair and solutions, reduces shame and blame and allows everyone involved to move on constructively.

Restorative practices have been used in schools around the world and when used consistently have been able to reduce overall conflict in school with better behavioural outcomes (Hansberry and Langley, 2013).

Riddles

Provide students with the 'Writing a riddle guide sheet'. Allow everyone five minutes to make up a riddle about an object in the classroom. Once students have come up with their riddle they write it on a piece of card. Keep the riddles handy to offer to the class throughout the weeks ahead as an opportunity to practise problem solving.

Treasure hunt

Each child is given a piece of 'treasure' and must hide it somewhere in the classroom or schoolyard. They must draw a map using pictures of the area complete with clues. Divide the class into pairs and allow them to each use problem solving to seek their partner's hidden treasure. Older students could use a riddle to find the treasure.

Work with one hand for an hour/day

Ask students to tuck one hand inside their top, keeping their dominant hand free. For the next hour they are challenged to go about their learning and so forth with only the use of one hand. They will encounter many opportunities for problem solving when they only have one hand available and will no doubt have fun in the process. You can make this even more challenging by getting them to tuck their dominant hand away instead!

Mental resilience activities

The following activities build mental resilience and can be offered each day as both an opportunity for problem solving and for building mental resilience. They are also great things to do while waiting for something:

1   Count backwards in twos from 110 (choose any number combinations depending on the age and ability of your students).
2   Spell the following list of words backwards in your head. For younger children: cat, the, in, as, me, to, it, car, dog, big, is, so, bit, was, go, on, for. For older students: beautiful, colour, laugh, joy, chicken, smile, funny, robot, little, school, science, garden, fishing, rainbow, birthday, dear, shopping, library, interesting.
3   Spell out the following words backwards and this time see who can say what the word is. For younger students: TAC, TAM, OT, TIB, OG, RAC, TOH, TIH, TON, TIS. For older students: ESIR, LLAF, REMMUS, TAOB, IKS, EFIL, RETNIW, SIRAP.
4   Write down or draw all your family members in a line from youngest to oldest including cousins, aunties, uncles and grandparents.
5   Ask students to arrange themselves as a class in a line from shortest to tallest.

Fingerprints

This activity takes some preparation and is best learnt by observing the teacher or a student modelling it first. All students will need to give a fingerprint of their index finger. Allow a variety of students to touch a few classroom windows, all of them creating fingerprints in different areas of the windows. (Do not allow numerous students to make a fingerprint in the same place.)

In small groups or pairs (depending on how many sets of fingerprints are there to explore), challenge students to dust the window for fingerprints. This is done by lightly dusting the window with talcum powder, blowing away the excess powder, then applying a piece of tape to the dusted fingerprint. Carefully peel the tape away from the window and stick it to a piece of black construction paper or poster board. The fingerprint is then taken to the display with all students' fingerprints and an attempt is made to solve whose print has been taken.

Puzzle me

Provide age-appropriate puzzles in pairs or small groups. Remind students that puzzles are all about problem solving – looking at the overall picture, coming up with possible solutions and trying solutions out until one fits. Puzzles take time and there is rarely a quick fix. This is great for developing patience and learning about trial and error.

Weekly challenge

(You might ask students to do this chapter's challenge over several weeks.)

Use the problem solving guide sheet and the plus and minus worksheet to solve one problem in each of the following areas. (For younger students only focus on one area and help them write it down in their journal.) If you don't have a problem in one of these areas then make one up!

1 Friendships
2 Home life
3 Chores/responsibilities
4 Learning
5 Fitness and health.

Parent tips

Use opportunities to try out problem solving

When your child comes home and tells you about a problem, ask them first what they think could resolve it. If you can, share simple problems you had at their age, and before you let them know how it was solved, ask them how they might have handled it. By having open discussions like this you provide your child with opportunities to problem solve in a safe and supported environment. You also normalise challenges and problems across generations.

Let your child speak and problem solve for themselves

Many parents rush in to help their child answer challenging questions – especially if their child is a little shy. The same parents might also do this when their child is experiencing a challenge or problem. Instead of guiding and encouraging their children to become confident and independent, they answer questions for their child, jump in and avoid situations where they feel their child might feel sad or disappointed. They try to fix their child's emotions so their child can feel happy all the time. Although this comes from love and the best of intentions it gives children the message, 'you need me to deal with life's challenges'. Being there as a source of guidance and encouragement allows your child to develop independence and problem solving skills.

Seek solutions

When you are faced with a problem, actively and openly seek solutions. Try not to get into the habit of complaining and blaming others or your situation for the problem. Show your child how courageous you can be and how active in seeking solutions. Do remember, however, some problems are not for children's ears. Choose what you share with your child carefully. They are children no matter how intelligent they are. They need the message the world is a safe and loving place, and the best place to learn that is through you at home.

Remain optimistic

Don't respond to problems your child brings home with angst. Give them a reassuring hug and tell them you are sure it will all work out. Encourage them to problem solve with your support and guidance and remind them life doesn't always go to plan and problems are an inevitable part of it. Show your child you have absolute faith in their ability to get through the problem.

Answer your child's questions with, 'what do you think?'

When your child asks you a question, help them develop problem solving skills by answering with, 'what do you think?' Give them a chance to try and work it out in your presence. Of course, there will be times when they just say, 'I don't know – that's why I am asking YOU!' and that's okay too of course. Not every interaction has to be a learning opportunity!

Avoid rescuing

From toddlerhood onwards the best learning occurs through play and experimentation. As long as your child is safe, let them work as much as possible out for themselves. Even though you will usually know a quicker, easier (and tidier!) way, try and avoid the temptation to step in. Instead, encourage, empathise and see what your child can come up with themselves. This is how problem solving confidence and skills build, not from observing you fixing them yourself.

Don't rush in to offer help

Although help seeking is very important for wellbeing and resilience, too much help seeking for things the child is capable of doing themselves is counterproductive. When your child is struggling with something, let them struggle as long as possible. As tempting as it can be to offer a hand or tell them what to do, do everything you can to wait and see what they come up with. Every time they help themselves they feel a sense of achievement and learn new skills. That sense of achievement makes them want to try new things again and problem solving becomes fun and exciting rather than stressful and worrying.

Create and cook your own recipes together

Create your own recipes and cooking styles together. No matter how good a chef you are, you are bound to make some mistakes. Quantities, ingredients, cooking temperatures and so forth are all important in how well a recipe turns out. If you have a go at creating together you will get plenty of chances to problem solve together – tasting your good, bad and uglies along the way!

Puzzles

Offer puzzles from an early age. Puzzles are brilliant for practising patience with problem solving, and they can be a great source of fun and relaxation. The more things your child practises solving, the more this ability will build in them.

BE THE BOSS OF PROBLEM SOLVING

Breathe **O**bserve **S**et a goal **S**eek solutions

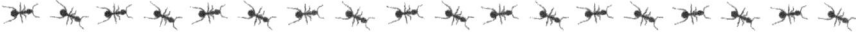

1: **B**REATHE to calm your brain.

2: **O**BSERVE. What is the problem? If someone else is part of the problem, what are they doing? If the problem is only to do with you, what can you see around you that might help solve this problem?

3: **S**ET A GOAL. How do you want this to turn out? If someone else is part of the problem, how might they want this to turn out?

4: **S**OLUTION SEEK. What can you try to solve this? Try it out. Did it work? If it didn't work, what else can you try?

Note to kids: Most problems have a solution. While it's good to problem solve on your own when you can, it's okay to talk through ideas with friends, family and teachers when you need extra help.

PROBLEM SOLVING
WORKING OUT THE PLUSES (ADVANTAGES/HELPFUL THINGS)
AND MINUSES (DISADVANTAGES/UNHELPFUL THINGS)

Breathe **O**bserve **S**et a goal **S**eek solutions

THE PROBLEM IS:

SOLUTION A:		SOLUTION B:	
Plus + :	Minus - :	Plus + :	Minus - :

SOLVING PROBLEMS WITH FRIENDS: GUIDE SHEET

1 **Breathe** and **focus** so you can think clearly.

2 **Ask** your friend, '**Can we talk** about what happened?'

3 If they are okay to talk, be ready to listen. Try not to think about what you want to say next. The questions below are a great place to start. You can wait to say what you think and feel until after your friend has spoken or you can give your own thoughts and feelings after each question. It really depends on how your friendship works through and what you both feel comfortable with.

'What do you think just happened between us?
I think _____ happened.'

'What are you thinking about this?'
('I'm thinking _____')

'What are you feeling?'
('I was feeling _____')

'How did I upset you?'
('I was upset when _____')

'What can I do to make things better?'
('I would feel much better if you _____')

4 **Show courage** and **say 'sorry'**. Saying 'sorry' doesn't mean that you are saying you are wrong. It can mean, 'sorry we are fighting' or 'sorry I hurt your feelings', or 'sorry things got messy between us'. It's a word we all know and when someone says 'sorry' to us, most of us feel better about that person and our relationship with them.

5 **Forgive** and **move on**. Staying mad at people for things they did never helps anyone. We are all learning and most of us are doing our best. There is no one in the world who has finished learning, and everyone makes mistakes. If the person keeps making the same mistake over and over, it is of course much harder to forgive. Let them know you are frustrated the same argument keeps happening. You might need to let an adult know and ask for their help. You might even want to spend time with other friends until things start working better between you and your friend.

If there's a disagreement or argument BOTH people or ALL people involved think they are right! That's why you're disagreeing! So it always pays to listen and put yourself in their shoes.

WRITING A RIDDLE: GUIDE SHEET

1   Start with the answer. Choose something to write about like an object or animal.

2   Think of clues to lead someone to guess it. If you were that thing, how would you describe yourself? Write them down.

3   Put the clues into short descriptive sentences such as:

■   I look like . . .

■   I sound like . . .

■   You see me . . .

■   I have . . .

■   I am . . .

■   I feel . . .

4   Be creative when you describe your answer. For example, if you are a diamond you might use descriptions like, 'I promise you forever' (diamonds are the strongest precious stone and said to last forever) and, 'You see me reign on golden circles' (diamonds are often put on the top of gold rings).

5   Once you have enough descriptions, try adding a sentence starting with 'BUT'. This is where you think of a way to use two opposing ideas. For example, if you were writing about the diamond you might say, 'I shine brighter than the sun by day' (diamonds are known for reflecting the sun and are really bright to the eyes) 'BUT can't be seen when the night is dark' (without light they can't reflect anything and blend into the darkness).

6   End your riddle with 'What am I?'

Reference list

Hansberry, B. and Langley, J. 2013. *The Grab and Go Circle Time Kit for Teaching Restorative Behaviour – 13 Sessions for Junior Primary*. Melbourne: Inyahead Publications.

Pearson, J. and Kordich Hall, D. 2008. 'Problem Solving Resource Sheet'. Ottawa: Canadian Child Care Foundation.

Seligman, M. 2007. *The Optimistic Child: A Proven Program to Safeguard Children Against Depression and Build Lifelong Resilience*. Sydney: Houghton Mifflin.

5 Keeping calm

Courage is fear holding on a minute longer.
George Patton

Introduction for education and health professionals

Stress and anxiety have always been part of the human experience, keeping us focused as well as safe from excessive risk or danger. Genetics, temperaments and past experiences help explain the difference in how much stress various people feel and take on board. Fluctuations in moods, energy levels and resilience follow accordingly.

During learning, transitions, conflict and changes, children's wellbeing and resilience may easily drop. The first step in helping students navigate their way through stress and anxiety is to take the mystery out of it. Naming it, normalising it and teaching children what to do about it helps them build courage from a young age to handle it constructively.

Stress triggers our primitive 'fight or flight' response giving a strong burst of adrenalin. This physiological aspect of stress can feel quite frightening when you don't understand what is happening. Adrenalin gives extra energy that can either be used for 'fight' (problem solving, solution seeking, physical exertion for stress relief), or 'flight' (avoiding the problem, keeping it cycling around in your head), or, in some situations, for 'freeze' (doing nothing and becoming paralysed with stress). Helping your students understand their stress response and teaching them useful things to do about it opens up neural pathways for coping. With practice these pathways become stronger and easier to use. Anyone who can handle stress well is bound for better wellbeing and resilience.

The role of the left and right amygdala is part of understanding stress and later in this chapter students will be given a chance to learn more about it. The amygdala is a primitive part of the brain dedicated to survival. It is the home of the 'fight or flight' response. Early humans owed their survival to the amygdala that kept them on high alert at all times for danger. Their brains were dedicated primarily to one thing – survival. When the amygdala detects a threat, it reacts quickly by releasing adrenalin for extra energy which makes the heart pump faster to get more blood and oxygen to the muscles – preparing you to fight, flee or freeze. The amygdala quickly surveys the perceived threat, communicates with other brain functions to seek previous experiences to provide more information, and then makes a decision about whether the situation is considered safe or unsafe. The body in response releases enough stress hormones to make you act quickly for self-preservation.

Humans have kept their amygdala throughout evolution because it helped them survive. The level of threat the amygdala was designed for in early humans is rarely of concern today. Even without the threat of sabre-toothed tigers, the amygdala is still quick to react to stress – before you can consciously think things through. That is why when faced with danger you might leap out of the way without even realising that is what you are doing. The amygdala's reaction is strong and significant. It takes over rational thinking and can consume the person with a larger than necessary reaction. The amygdala not only reacts to real stressors – it reacts to perceived stressors. This is particularly challenging for young people with anxiety who have a tendency to over-react to stress and find themselves in 'fight, flight or freeze' more often than necessary.

Developing skills to manage stress from an early age is much easier than teaching those skills later when unhelpful habits may have become embedded. If you do wait to teach these skills until there is an obvious challenge, there is the added difficulty for the student to learn something new while feeling stressed and under pressure.

Explanation for younger students

Stress happens when things don't go as planned or when you are worried about something and don't know what to do. The problem can be small, like forgetting your hat and not being allowed to play outside at playtime, or your teacher being away sick. Or, it can be bigger, like moving house, changing schools, or fighting a lot with a friend or someone you love. Stress gets worse when you don't know what to do about it. It gets especially bad when the thing that's making you stressed doesn't get better and keeps happening, like not having anyone to play with day after day. That can make you feel stressed. Or, not understanding the school work and feeling left behind. Stress can get bigger if you keep it inside and don't tell anyone about it. Stress makes your body feel different too. Your heart beats faster, you might feel hot, and your breathing can get really fast. Stress can even feel scary. The good news is that stress can help keep you on track about what is important to you, and all those scary feelings like your pumping heart are actually giving you extra energy to handle whatever is bothering you. You will learn how over the next few weeks.

Explanation for older students

Stress is a feeling you get when things feel bigger in your life than you can handle. When you are stressed you feel like there is just too much to think about. Challenges with friends and family, school work, sports practice and studying for tests all take up a lot of energy. When you're stressed your brain sends out signals that there is a problem. Your body releases adrenalin and makes your heart pump faster, which can make you feel really awful. This extra energy can make you over-react (fight), or under-react (flight or freeze), or actually be used for courage to rise up to the challenge in front of you. Stress can get big quickly if you don't problem solve or ask for help. Keeping stressful feelings inside you may make stress worse. There are many things you can try to avoid stress building up, and to beat stress when it lands on your doorstep. You're certainly not alone if you feel stressed. Stress is a normal reaction to keeping up with life's challenges.

Someone who kept calm:

Mackenzie Bearup, founder of Sheltering Books Inc.: keeping calm during pain through reading

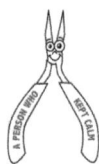

Mackenzie Bearup is the founder of 'Sheltering Books Inc.', who give away books to disadvantaged children in homeless shelters in the hope of igniting their love for reading. When she was only 11 years old, Mackenzie was diagnosed with Complex Regional Pain Syndrome. Her left knee swelled up badly and that was the start of a lifelong battle with incurable pain. She likens her pain to 'a bomb going off in my knee', and at times the pain has been so excruciating she has had to spend months off her feet in bed. So many strong feelings emerged: anger, resentment, frustration, loneliness and boredom. Mackenzie says immersing herself in a book was what helped her keep calm and cope with her pain. One day she heard about the Murphy Harpst

---

Children's Center in Cedartown, Georgia, a home for some of the most abused children in the country. They had built a library, but had no books. Mackenzie set a goal to fill that library. She knew these young people would be finding it difficult to keep calm and cope with life and she hoped the joy of reading would bring them some relief. By sending out flyers and telling anyone who would listen, she filled their library to capacity at 11,000 books! She is now close to having donated almost 40,000 books to disadvantaged young people. Mackenzie believes a love of reading contributes to a love of learning and hopes that if disadvantaged youth can be inspired to stay at school this gives them a much better chance of staying out of trouble later down the track.

GROUP DISCUSSION AND BRAINSTORM

Central concept: stress

- What is stress?
- Is stress normal?
- What makes stress bigger?
- What makes stress smaller?
- Is something wrong with you if you get stressed?

Our class stress bar graph

What makes people stressed? Students share what stresses them out. Record the answers or place each stressor on a bright card to add later to the 'stress less' poster activity later in the chapter.

Possible answers may include 'school work, friendships, getting in trouble at school, forgetting something, conflict with parents, feeling lonely, too many things to do, people fighting, homework' and so forth.

After the brainstorm create a bar graph showing how many people in the class share each stress by asking students to raise their hand as you go through each stressor. Use this as an opportunity to normalise the experience of stress, reminding students that life has its challenges and everyone feels overwhelmed sometimes.

Life focused on survival

A short conversation with your students . . .

A long time ago when the first humans lived in caves, things could get scary very quickly. Dangerous predators were everywhere on the lookout for their next meal. The first human brains were built with an amazing part called an AMYGDALA (ah-mig-der-la). The amygdala sensed danger quickly and reacted fast to give the human the best chance of surviving. When the amygdala sensed danger it ordered the body to pump out adrenalin, so the heart would beat faster, getting blood out to the muscles. This encouraged the humans to become stronger and faster so they could survive an attack from something or someone scary.

As the amygdala did such a great job at helping humans survive, it stayed throughout the brain's evolution even though dangers like lions and tigers diminished and life became much safer. The amygdala is one of the most primitive parts of our brains today and remains unchanged from early human history. Here's the problem – the amygdala is over-reactive. If the amygdala thinks you are in danger (in other words if YOU THINK you are in danger), it believes you, and so begins the FIGHT–FLIGHT response. It gets set to battle, run away or be frozen in fear and do nothing. It also switches off your logical thinking.

In the schoolyard the 'fight' bit may look like someone hitting back when they get knocked over. The 'flight' bit may look like someone running away when teased. Neither response is very helpful today – unless of course you are in serious danger, which you very rarely are. When all of this is going on, your body feels a bit out of control. This is what it feels like to be in fight, flight or freeze mode. Once you understand that this is your stress response – not you – you can take steps to calm your body down.

Let's look at what happens to you in class when you feel worried, stressed or under threat. What does your fight or flight response feel like? Many students find their heart beats faster, their stomach feels tight, or they feel sick and sweat more. Falling asleep may be a struggle among those with concentration difficulties. Headaches can be a problem as well as changes in your appetite, like not wanting to eat or feeling hungry all the time – often for salty, sugary and processed foods.

Fill in your early warning sign worksheet to show how your body feels when you are stressed. You can write what you feel in the corresponding body part or shade in where you feel stress.

Early warning sign: worksheet

Hand out the early warning sign ('My body when it's not calm') worksheet found at the end of this chapter. Talk to students about how our bodies react to our thoughts and feelings. Many students find it difficult to remember what they physically feel in association with stress. If this is the case, you can either ask them to try and imagine what it feels like, or ask them to fill the warning sheet out at a later time after paying more focused attention to that feeling next time they are under stress.

'I can handle it': calming ideas worksheet

Hand out the worksheet found at the end of the chapter as a quick reference guide for de-stressing.

The stress less goal setting challenge (for older students)

Now your students have some tricks to manage stress it's time to give them a chance to set goals around it. In their journals ask them to write a short plan about where they want to feel less stressed, what might get in their way and how they will deal with things getting in their way.

My stress less plan (worksheet for older students)

Hand out the worksheet found at the end of the chapter to help students set goals around managing their stress.

Breathing exercises

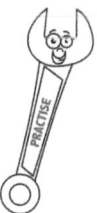

Breathing in oxygen and breathing out carbon dioxide through diaphragmatic breathing lowers blood pressure and slows your heartbeat, calming the nerves. Teaching young children to breathe in slowly and deeply gives them a skill they can control easily, and the benefits far outweigh the effort involved in developing the skill.

Young children might enjoy blowing on a pinwheel, watching it spin slowly as they learn to control the breath. Bubble blowing also relies on blowing slowly and gently (otherwise the bubbles may pop or not form at all). Older students can pretend they're blowing up a balloon inside their tummy as they watch their belly grow through the diaphragmatic breath. Once they understand how to control their breathing, teach them a variety of relaxing breathing exercises.

How big does this rate? Keeping things in perspective

Hand out the 'How big does this rate? From ants to dinosaurs' worksheet found at the end of this chapter. The idea is to relate the size of a worry to the size of the animal so students develop perspective around challenges. Reflecting on the size of a challenge and keeping things in perspective can help young people manage stress successfully (Fischer et al., 2011).

Remind students there are no right or wrong answers as you ask them to rate each worry from the list below with an animal. If you notice patterns such as some students rating a problem like leaving their hat at home as a dinosaur, then check their understanding again and help them gain perspective about the gravity of various difficulties.

Problems to offer students to rate

You left your hat at home. You are not allowed in the yard at break time or lunch.

You came last in a race again.

You have a lot of homework to do and you are really tired.

You don't understand what the teacher has just explained to the class.

Your best friend says they don't like you anymore.

Your team keeps losing at soccer.

You are being bullied.

Your school evacuation bell rings.

You've fallen off the monkey bars and you are in a lot of pain.

Your parents are late to pick you up.

You have lost your favourite thing.

You are sick and will miss out on the school disco.

You have arrived at school on casual day in your uniform.

You have lost something you promised to take care of for your friend.

You came to school without your lunch today.

You are learning to roller skate. Everyone else is learning faster than you.

You can't find your consent form for a school excursion. The excursion is today.

You broke your mum's favourite vase.

You didn't wear a jumper to school and it's really cold.

You took something that belongs to someone else.

You failed a test at school.

Your parents are mad at you for something you feel really ashamed of.

You've lost a school library book.

You've been hit by another child.

You found something in the yard that doesn't belong to you and you really want to keep it.

Introducing mindfulness: a note to the facilitator

The practice of mindfulness (being completely and non-judgementally engaged in what you are doing in the present moment) is not easy in today's fast-paced world. Teaching your students to practise mindfulness will build their resilience and wellbeing as they learn to slow down and enjoy the moment without thinking about what will be happening next or what might go wrong.

Learning to be mindful can encourage the brain into an 'approach' state where you are comfortable about facing your challenges rather than avoiding them. In other words, your brain wires for resilience (Siegel, 2010).

The 'smiling mind' App is an excellent way to begin the journey of mindfulness in your classroom. The App teaches good meditation practice and guides students about how to be more mindful.

In your classroom you may wish to model mindfulness and engage in mindfulness activities such as meditation, nature observation walks and gratitude practice. When a student is having a difficult time, you can help bring them back into the moment, encouraging them to stay focused on what they are doing right here and now. Some time outdoors to be mindful, observing and listening to nature, can help many students calm down and clear their minds.

Worksheet: 'I can handle it' calming ideas

Hand out the calming ideas from the 'I can handle it' worksheet found at the end of the chapter. Allow students some time to circle as many calming techniques as they would like to try.

Expect the best: positive visualisation exercise

The subconscious mind can be fooled into thinking you are doing something just by imagining it or telling yourself you can do it. It believes everything you tell it, unlike the conscious mind (Smalley, 2013). The more you imagine yourself doing something, the stronger the connections you make in your brain (as if you're actually doing it for real). Ask students to think of their greatest fear. It might be talking in front of the class, attending a new activity, climbing something high, or standing up to a bully. Offer a few rounds of 4–7–8 breathing and ask students to imagine the challenging situation. Next, they see themselves handling the situation with confidence. 'Continue slow breathing. Allow yourself to do this many times and let your brain create pathways for success by imagining success. Build on those pathways by actually challenging yourself to deal with that situation just as you have visualised.' While doing the visualisation, students encourage themselves by telling themselves, 'I can do this well.'

Role plays: 'Help a friend'

In the following role plays, students can practise their understanding about stress and worry by helping a friend, using the framework below.

Framework for talking to someone who is stressed

1 Ask, 'Are you okay?'
2 Listen (that means no talking or suggestions!)
3 Say, 'I know how you feel' or 'That's hard/sad/horrible'
4 Say, 'I want to help/I'm here for you/Is there something I can do?'

Role play scenarios (in pairs or small groups)

1 Your friend tells you someone they love is really sick.

2 Your friend tells you they have no one to play with at school.

3 Your friend tells you about how they are being bullied.

4 Your friend doesn't understand a lot of the school work.

5 Your friend is feeling stressed because their parents are arguing a lot.

6 Your friend wants to go on school camp but their parents don't have the money to pay for it.

7 Your friend really wants a pet but their parents say, 'no pets'.

8 Your friend wants to change schools.

9 Your friend has to move house and they don't like the new house at all.

10 Your friend is leaving the school.

11 Your friend has lost their wallet at school.

12 Your friend has been asked to go to the principal's office after lunch. They don't know why.

13 Your friend is feeling unfit and unhealthy.

14 Your friend has left their homework at home.

Guided meditation

Imagining beautiful places and indulging the senses is a great way to de-stress and foster resilience and wellbeing. Offer the imagined scene below or a personal favourite. Encourage your students to bring their own in as well. Allowing guided meditation into your classroom as regular practice builds wellbeing in you and your students.

You see an old wooden door at the back of your garden. You haven't seen this door before. You open it and all around you are beautiful trees, higher than you have ever seen before. You've never seen so much green. It's warm. The breeze gently dances on your skin. The sun shines playfully between the leaves on the trees, casting the most amazing shadows all around you.

A bird gently nudges its babies from the nest. They are ready to learn to fly. One by one they pop in and out of the nest, each time flying for just a little longer. A butterfly surprises you by landing on your shoulder. You wait quietly, wondering what she will do next. She stays for a while. Then just as you soak in her glorious colours she flies off into the distance.

A caterpillar crunches through a crisp green leaf. Delicious. You wonder if the butterfly you saw started from a caterpillar like the one you just enjoyed. As the caterpillar disappears from sight you notice the most amazing spider web you have ever seen. It has been crafted carefully between two pine trees. The sun is dancing along the web as the smallest drops of dew settle all over it. The spider finally takes a rest as it watches over its creation.

Suddenly you hear the leaves rustling behind you. As you move your gaze you see the sweetest little animal you have ever seen. Big bright eyes look up at you as it sees you take notice. It jumps up and seems to offer you a little dance. In a moment, the tiny creature is gone, just as quickly as it came. You like it here. You decide to stay for a while. Lying on a bed of leaves you take some deep, warm, gentle breaths. You are grateful for finding this place.

Write your own guided meditation

Students can enjoy having a go at writing their own visualisation using the framework below. Younger students will enjoy drawing their special place using the framework as a guide on what to include.

Guided meditation framework

1 Think of a place you imagine would be relaxing.
2 What can you see?
3 What can you hear?
4 What can you smell?
5 Is it warm? Cold? Dark? Bright?
6 Is there a breeze or is it still?

A guided meditation is not easy to write and can take a few drafts to perfect. Allow this if possible. Once all your students have created their own guided meditation, consider making it into a classroom (or even school library) resource.

Introducing 'flow': a note to facilitators

'Flow' is simply the sense of being so engaged in a goal-oriented activity that you lose sense of time and space. You are involved for the intrinsic pleasure of the activity. Once you have reached your goal, you feel so satisfied it is likely that you will seek more opportunities in the area to immerse in further states of flow. It is important to know 'flow' cannot be rushed into and out of. It sometimes takes time after starting an activity to engage in the experience of flow – and sometimes getting started itself is the hardest part (Csikszentmihalyi, 2008).

What is 'flow'?

A short conversation with your students . . .

Ask students whether they have ever heard sports people talk about being in 'the zone'? Flow is similar to the 'zone'. It is a state you get into when you want to do something, and while you do it you feel completely absorbed, losing track of time and place. Flow often happens the most when you're active or creative. Flow supports your wellbeing and resilience. When you have activities in your life that regularly bring you flow, you feel more relaxed, happy and mentally strong.

Going with the 'flow' survey

Hand out the 'Going with the "flow" survey' at the end of this chapter. For younger students the survey can be read out.

Embrace challenge

Provide students with a variety of puzzles to solve in pairs or small groups. Target the puzzles at a level you feel your students will find easy (make sure you consider the differing developmental levels of your students when grouping and selecting puzzles). Listen to the dialogue between the students and write down anything you hear that is relevant to how students react to finding things too easy (comments like, 'this is boring', 'this is too easy' and so forth).

Now present students with a puzzle one step above what you feel they are capable of. One of the foundations of flow is engaging in an activity that is challenging at one level above your current abilities (Csikszentmihalyi, 2008). Observe the students' reactions and comments, recording these also. Talk to students afterwards about which puzzle they enjoyed doing more and discuss the value of working on projects that challenge us and push us to a new level of learning. Where possible, generalise this approach to all your students' learning and try and keep them challenged. Avoid making challenges too difficult and out of their reach, though, as this will cause anxiety and more frustration than is useful for creating 'flow' and learning through 'flow'.

And the secret ingredient is . . .

Ask students to invent a recipe. There are only two rules for their invention:

1   The recipe must have one element of surprise – something you wouldn't usually expect to have with the other ingredients.
2   The recipe must be new to the person writing it. It must not be a recipe they already know.

Encourage students to try their recipes at home and they might even wish to bring a small sample in to class to share. You might also consider doing this in small groups and allowing the class to cook at school and test out their recipes.

Class playlist

Music helps you relax and connect with others. Provide each student with three small pieces of card or paper. Invite them to write down a favourite singer or song on each piece of paper. The music must be upbeat and positive in order to work as an energiser and de-stressor. Collect the papers and agree to create a playlist of positive music representing class favourites. Try and play songs from the playlist each day when silence is not necessary for learning. At other times relaxing classical music in the classroom can help relax excited nerves. Students can also help create this playlist.

Positive words jar

Open a class brainstorm to create a list of positive words. Write them down and place them in a jar, allowing students to take one word out a day. Write the word clearly for all to see and use it to reflect on as much as you can through the day. Encourage students to act and learn in ways that can be described by that word.

Make a 'to do' list

If you have ever felt overwhelmed and decided to write a 'to do' list you probably know how much it helps you feel less stressed. Just getting everything out onto paper often helps you see what you need to get done. Provide students with a small piece of paper and ask them to write their own 'to do' lists to display at home on their fridge (or you can have a 'to do' board where students set their weekly list of 'to dos' and tick them off on completion). If you are able to encourage students to do this each week, you will help them manage their workloads at school and chores at home.

Laugh

As a homework exercise, ask students to find three jokes they have never heard before. The challenge is that they are not to find these online. They must find them by asking others or looking in joke books. After checking with a parent that the joke is suitable to share with their class, ask students to bring in their jokes and add them to the joke jar prepared earlier by you. Make it a morning and/or afternoon ritual to read a joke to the class. Laughter is a wonderful way to de-stress and it connects a group.

Balloon push

This activity is best done in a large space. To further explore how stress feels, hand out a balloon to each student. Once their balloon is blown up, provide permanent markers so students can write on it what they get stressed or worried about, e.g. losing something special, being late, coming last, not understanding school work, homework or being too busy.

   As students often become excited when they are around balloons, start by offering them a chance to play 'balloon tennis'. In pairs they simply throw their balloons back and forth to each other. Using one balloon per pair is easiest but throwing both is a fun challenge.

After the students have released their excitement, bring them back to the circle. Remind them you are exploring stress today. Ask them how they felt after the game of balloon tennis. Energised? Relaxed? Excited? Talk about how these feelings are released through exercise, which is one of the best stress busters around.

Holding your balloon up, gently press it between your hands or against something. Talk about how stress is another word for 'pressure'. When we are stressed we feel pushed. We feel like more is happening than we can handle. We sometimes feel like we could burst! Ask students to imagine they are going to burst their stresses away and allow them to push on their balloons until they pop. This can be a great way to show they are releasing their stress. (Some students struggle with balloon popping. If this is the case, avoid the popping component.)

Feelings on the spot

Throughout the week spontaneously ask the class to draw (or older students might prefer to write) how they are feeling, 'right now', in their journal. This activity doesn't need to take much time and it allows students to become more aware of their changing moods. Normalise these fluctuations and just how many different feelings show their face from one hour to the next. Being aware of this also helps students not take their moods too seriously and to keep perspective that everything passes with time.

Progressive muscle relaxation

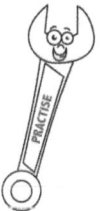

When you feel stressed, your fight–flight reaction makes your muscles tense. Progressive muscle relaxation allows you to tense all your muscle groups in sequence and release the tension as you let go. Your body feels more relaxed and your mind soon follows. Many young children find it difficult to develop this skill and some benefit from trying something like isometrics first (where you use an object to create resistance instead of creating the tension independently). For example, the child might push their body against a wall and hold for 20 seconds, then push their legs up against the wall and hold. Other ways to encourage tensing and relaxing the muscles for a similar benefit are jumping on a trampoline, bike riding, rock climbing, roller skating, going to a gym, punching a punching bag, swimming and running.

Progressive muscle relaxation sequence

(Hold muscles tight for 10 seconds and release them for 10 to 20 seconds before going on to the next muscle.)

Lie on the floor and close your eyes. Notice how your body is feeling right now.

Take in three slow deep breaths, breathing in through your nose and out slowly through tight lips.

Lift your eyebrows up as high as you can and hold . . . now release.

Smile widely like a clown in a sideshow alley and hold . . . now release.

Lift your shoulders up high like you're trying to touch your ears and hold . . . now release.

Straighten out your arms making a fist at the end and hold . . . now release.

Push your arms back against the floor like you're trying to push the floor away from you and hold . . . now release.

Squeeze your bottom as tight as you can and hold . . . now release.

Tighten your thighs up and hold . . . now release.

Pull your feet towards you so your calf muscles grow tight and hold . . . now release.

Lift your arms up over your head and push your feet downwards making yourself as tall as you can and hold . . . now release.

REPEAT one to three more times, asking students to pay attention to how their body feels at the end compared to the beginning.

This can be followed by a guided meditation or visualisation.

Silent bird count

Take your students outside and once they are comfortable begin a 2–5-minute period of silence. Their goal is to listen to the birds and try to differentiate the different bird calls. They must all try and gather how many different birds they heard. There is of course no way of knowing the right answer, because some will listen and notice better than others. Watch your students enjoy repeating the calls they heard and enjoy the benefits to their wellbeing as they spend focused time on a relaxing activity.

Silence is bliss

Inject periods during the school day where students are encouraged to observe and enjoy complete silence. This is a playful activity that many students will find particularly difficult. When silence is broken, it is important to be kind but firm about it. Ask your students to respect the silence as if it were something sacred. To symbolise a period of quiet in the class you may wish to turn off the lights and turn on a soft lamp, or use a candle or fairy lights instead. You can offer bursts of silence that last anywhere between five minutes and an hour. You can even make this into a challenge and set a goal to be able to achieve an hour of silence as a class by a certain time. Reward the students with something when they reach their goal. Make sure you also talk with the students about how difficult maintaining silence is and what the challenges as well as benefits are.

Clay balls

Provide students with their own small piece of modelling clay. Let them know they are able to hold this small piece of clay and fidget with it any time they feel stressed. Some students will find the opportunity very exciting and want to use it more often than necessary. Usually the novelty wears off and they are able to regulate their use of the clay. If necessary you could place a limit on when the clay can be taken out and how it can be used. The repetitive movements and sensing with the fingertips associated with clay modelling play are very relaxing for many people and can act as an additional stress regulator when used daily.

Weekly challenge

Ask your students to journal one thing they feel stressed by. Younger students might draw it. Divide them into pairs and ask them to decide on a stress reducing method in the week ahead to see if it helps. Make sure the pairs talk again at the end of the challenge to discuss if their plan was useful and to think about what they could try instead if their stress continues to be a concern.

Parent tips

Acknowledge stress

Without sharing information that is not age-appropriate, allow the word 'stress' in your home. Talk about how everyone feels under pressure from time to time, and when your child seems stressed, let them know you can see they're having a tough time. You might even like to have a family de-stress day (and call it that) when you feel your family becoming overloaded. Do something out of your routine that everyone has been wanting to do for a while, and say how important time together away from stress is.

When you are able to appropriately share your stressful experiences, your child can see how different people handle and respond to stress. Your message should always be that you are okay and taking measures to find solutions and manage your stress.

There are also positive and useful aspects to stress that are worth sharing with your children. Stress provides energy thanks to all that adrenalin pumping through your system. Muscles work harder and faster, your reaction times speed up and, if it is paired with focus, self-encouragement and confidence, stress can actually improve performance!

Encourage your child to take deep slow breaths

This chapter has a number of breathing exercises to use at home as well. Try them out and model them when you are feeling stressed.

Use progressive muscle relaxation

Use the progressive muscle relaxation sequence provided in this chapter to help children fall asleep more easily or to prepare for a challenging event. A relaxed mind usually follows a relaxed body. Older children benefit from gym work that exerts their muscles, providing them with a similar sense of release.

Show confidence in your child

When your child is going through any difficult period, show confidence that they will get through it. While it's important to acknowledge and empathise, it is equally important to be solution-focused and optimistic. Always look forward to the challenging period passing and emphasise that it will.

Avoid rescuing your child from their mistakes

Your child's mistakes are a normal part of development. Mistakes lead to learning and are an important step in their developing self-esteem, confidence and emotional regulation. Try and allow them to experience mistakes in a safe and supportive environment so they learn mistakes are a natural part of life. Supporting them to do as much as possible for themselves when problem solving or handling a mistake helps build their confidence and resilience. Young people need to know they can handle life's stressors without relying on you to 'fix' them. Whenever possible, give them the chance to make mistakes without feeling shame or blame and to face the natural consequences of their actions. If you resign yourself to walking on eggshells around a child with a sensitive temperament, they will learn to control you through their anxiety. Sensitive children, like all children, need to experience the range of emotions and learn how to handle disappointment, anxiety and frustration, even though it might take them much longer to learn this than their more even-tempered peers.

Hug!

Hugs release oxytocin – a hormone that makes us feel deeply connected to others, improving our sense of wellbeing and relaxation. Cuddling pets works too!

Count your blessings

Help your children notice all the wonderful gifts each day can bring. Finding a special rock, seeing a rainbow, something funny, something delicious – there are so many small gifts in our days. Practise noticing them with your children and, when you can, just stop and look. Soak it in and enjoy it. When your children see you stopping and noticing you will soon find them doing the same. For more on gratitude, see Chapter 1, 'Gratitude, perspective and optimism'.

Practise mindfulness

Mindfulness is about being fully engaged in the present moment. Slowing down enough to be present is one step closer to resilience. When you are fully engaged in what is going on around you and you have a deeper awareness of what you are feeling, you are less likely to want to control situations when they go against your expectations. The 'smiling mind' App is a great way to bring mindfulness into your home. Other ways include giving your child your complete attention when having a conversation, enjoying mindful hugs and cuddles, turning off devices during family time, cloud watching, taking a walk, and immersing and celebrating the senses.

Encourage a balanced diet

Help your children learn about eating well to think, play and learn. Offer interesting fresh foods and let them choose at least one or two fruits and vegetables for the family to try when they join you shopping. Nutritious food feeds and energises the brain in ways that contribute to wellbeing.

Explore creativity together

Take on a creative pursuit together. Buy a large canvas and paint it together, sew together, decorate a room, landscape your garden, do a mosaic, learn origami – anything that allows everyone to be involved and create something new together. These experiences build long-lasting memories for your family and if they are something that can be hung up, worn or used they will be a frequent reminder of a special time together.

Label feelings from an early age and show empathy

Help your child know the names of the wide array of feelings they experience. Next time they are unhappy about something, instead of encouraging them to cheer up, try labelling their feelings and showing empathy. If your child comes last in the race, instead of wishing them better luck next time, you can try, 'You are so disappointed. You wanted to win so much. That's a big feeling to handle.' This exploration of feelings makes feelings less scary and mysterious and reduces anxiety.

Encourage flow

Home life can become too busy sometimes. Try and offer uninterrupted unstructured time every weekend to help your child enjoy a state of 'flow'. (The 'Going with the flow' survey will give you some ideas about what you could do.) The more time your child spends engaging in activities that they can become totally immersed in, the happier and more relaxed they will feel. Spending time in 'flow' increases wellbeing and resilience.

Also remember, interrupting 'flow' can be intensely frustrating for anyone and many tantrums from children transitioning from one activity to another are a result of 'flow' being interrupted. So if you're going to offer some time for your child to enjoy a 'flow'-inducing activity, try and avoid a time where there is something to get to or do soon afterwards.

Practise silence

Schedule ten minutes, one hour or even half a day one weekend to dedicate to silence. Turn it into a game. Ask your children, 'how long do you think you can stay quiet for?' and 'who do you think can be the quietest for the longest?' Have fun with it! This is a great challenge to do outdoors where nature helps calm excited nerves. When you do end the silence, celebrate your achievement with a silly song or game together.

Try yoga as a family

This ancient method of stress management and overall body relaxation is a moving meditation. It gives everyone a chance to breathe well and be mindful of their body as you focus on a variety of poses. Sun salutations are fun and easy and as your family get used to it you can add more to your repertoire.

Sing together

Most children love to sing. What's even better is they really don't realise how bad your singing is until they're much older! Singing together, sharing your favourite songs while they share theirs, is a great way to connect and relax together. Let your children create a family top 10 or 20 where everyone can add their songs. When you sing you are focused and concentrate on just singing. You breathe deeply and fully. The music playing relaxes and energises you too.

Massage

Have fun with family nights in where the tone is set for massage, quiet music and candles. Take turns in giving each other a gentle massage and make sure everyone knows this is an optional activity. Giving someone else a massage is an act of love and kindness. Receiving it from someone is deeply connecting. Massage also creates better body awareness as children work out what feels good and what doesn't. Allowing your children to choose the scent they like is another way to relax and connect.

Nature play

Spend as much time as possible as a family outdoors. Children tend to argue less with each other when they're outside in the fresh air exploring. Nature Play SA (https://natureplaysa.org.au/) has a brilliant selection of ideas for young and old that brings out all the best nature has to offer. Try and have a go at an outdoor family adventure each weekend – even if it is simply a ten-minute birdwatching walk after work around your neighbourhood.

Bring nature indoors

Bringing beautiful things your children find in nature inside your home to enjoy is another way to gain the benefits the outdoors has to offer. Provide your children with a small display tray where they can add things they find outside that are pleasing to the eye. Enjoy them for a few days before allowing new ones in. Enjoy the conversations that follow as children marvel at the shapes and colours given by nature and try to work out what place their treasure has in the broad scheme of nature.

MY BODY WHEN IT'S NOT CALM

Draw/colour/write in what happens to your body when it's not calm.

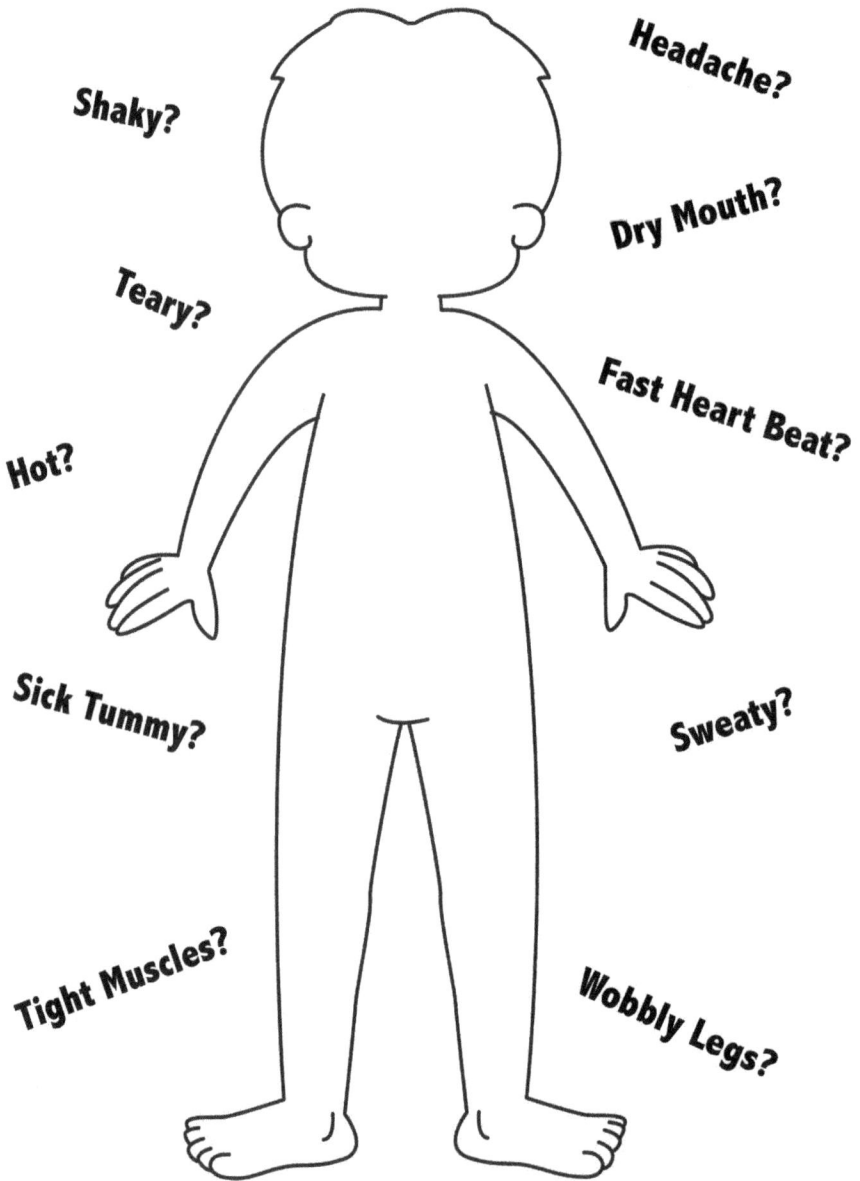

Shaky?

Headache?

Dry Mouth?

Teary?

Fast Heart Beat?

Hot?

Sick Tummy?

Sweaty?

Tight Muscles?

Wobbly Legs?

'I CAN HANDLE IT'
CALMING IDEAS

Circle all the calming ideas you like from the list. Choose at least 5. This list will remind you there are lots of things to do that are calming. Try one next time you're not calm. Younger students can draw a list of calming ideas after the ideas have been explained to them verbally.

1. Breathe slowly and deeply

2. Go outside

3. Do something kind for someone else

4. Imagine something or someone you love

5. Read a joke book

6. Be around friends

7. Ride a bike

8. Play with a ball

9. Look at photos

12. Cloud watch

13. Play with a pet

14. Draw

15. Read

16. Make a cubby

17. Garden

18. Cook

19. Build or create something

20. Talk to a friend on the phone

21. Skype a friend

22. Meditate

23. Encourage yourself, 'I can handle this' and 'I have courage' and 'this will all work out in the end'

24. Notice 3 things you are thankful for right now

MY STRESS LESS PLAN

1   WHAT DO YOU FEEL STRESSED ABOUT? Homework? Learning? Jobs at home? Friendships? What you are eating? Arguments with family members?

2   WHAT DO YOU WANT TO FEEL INSTEAD? (On top of homework? Like you understand the work? That you are keeping up with your jobs at home? That you're getting along with your friends? You're eating healthily and you have more energy? That you are getting along well with family members?)

3   WHAT MIGHT BE THE CHALLENGE GETTING IN YOUR WAY? Too much to do every day? Not understanding school work? Distractions? Wanting to do something instead? Feeling tired? Having trouble handling your feelings? Finding it hard to take responsibility for your actions but feeling guilty that you know you have done the wrong thing?

4   WHAT CAN YOU DO ABOUT THE CHALLENGE? Ask for help? Write a 'to do' list, and put it on your calendar? Use the things you want to do more as a reward for finishing the challenge? Make a decision to learn how to handle your feelings better? Get more sleep? Find courage to take responsibility for all your actions?

5   IMAGINE YOURSELF HANDLING YOUR STRESS WELL. What does it feel like when you are less stressed about this? How do you feel about beating the challenge?

HOW BIG DOES THIS RATE?
FROM ANTS TO DINOSAURS

ANT (1) Something **small** has gone wrong. **I can handle it on my own.**

STICK INSECT (2) Something **bigger** has gone wrong. **Talking/drawing or writing** about it **should help make it better.**

BEARDED DRAGON (3) Something **huge** has gone wrong. **I am thinking about it a lot.** I need someone else to know about it and **I need help** to find a solution.

CROCODILE (4) Something **humongous** has gone wrong. I can't think about anything else. **My body feels awful.** I can't enjoy what I am doing and I probably won't be able to sleep. **I don't feel comfortable. I need help soon.**

DINOSAUR (5) Something **mammoth** has gone wrong. **I need help straight away** so things can be safe.

GOING WITH THE 'FLOW' SURVEY

Circle what you feel excited and energised by.
If you have to think about it for a while, it probably isn't something you find 'flow' in.

Inventing	Playing an instrument
Learning new things	Listening to music
Adventures	Helping others
Making a space look beautiful	Reading
Camping	Talking to people
Fishing	Listening to people
Researching	Playing sport
Martial arts	Watching sport
Collecting	Being active
Writing stories	Painting/drawing
Writing poems	Dancing
Cooking	Gardening
Science	Cleaning
Competing	Roller skating
Acting/drama	Rock climbing
Singing	Craft

6 TRICKS TO KEEP CALM

Try an idea from below next time you need to calm down. Rate how helpful it was.

5/5 = problem solved
4/5 = much better
3/5 = mostly better
2/5 = a bit better
1/5 = a tiny bit better
0/5 = no better

Trick 1: Breathe slowly. Breathing slowly calms your brain.

Trick 2: 4-7-8 breathing. Breathe in slowly through your nose for 4 seconds, hold your breath for 7 seconds then breathe out slowly through tight lips for 8 seconds. Repeat 3 times.

Trick 3: Encourage yourself. Talk to yourself like you would talk to a friend having a tough time. Try, 'I will get through this', or 'this is tough but I'm tougher' or 'I have courage to handle most things.' Encouraging yourself is healthy for your brain and it grows confident and helpful thinking patterns.

Trick 4: Get some energy out by being active, doing progressive muscle relaxation or by talking to someone. Writing and drawing about your feelings can help too.

Trick 5: Eat and drink healthily. The food and drink that goes into your body can give you useful energy to think, play, learn and sleep well. Or it can give you unhelpful energy 'highs' and 'lows' that make you think, play, learn and sleep badly. Eat as much fresh, healthy food as you can and keep those sugary, salty foods for sometimes.

Trick 6: Sleep enough. A good night's sleep helps you recover from your day – bringing you more energy for the next day.

WHAT MAKES ME ANGRY?

Feeling angry makes extra energy. Tick anything here that makes you feel angry. When that thing happens again, try a calming idea to help you feel better.

I FEEL ANGRY WHEN...

☐ I have to do something I don't want to do

☐ I have to go somewhere I don't want to go

☐ People argue around me

☐ I feel left out

☐ I hear someone say something bad about me

☐ I get teased

☐ Someone touches my things without asking

☐ No one seems to have time to listen to me

☐ Other people make decisions for me without asking what I think

☐ Someone makes a promise and breaks it

☐ I don't understand the school work

☐ I make a mistake

☐ Someone else breaks the rules

☐ I can't get something I really want

☐ Someone says, 'no' and I want them to say 'yes', or at least, 'maybe!'

WHAT I DO WHEN I AM ANGRY

Tick what you do when you are angry.

☐ **Scream or shout**

☐ **Yell**

☐ **Storm out of the room**

☐ **Stomp my feet**

☐ **Cry**

☐ **Say mean things to the person**

☐ **Make threats (if you don't do X I will X)**

☐ **Glare/stare at who I am mad at**

☐ **Stop listening**

☐ **Say things I later regret**

☐ **Try and make the other person feel bad/guilty**

☐ **Ignore everyone**

Write down 3 things you could do with that energy instead.

1. _____

_____

_____

2. _____

_____

_____

3. _____

_____

_____

Reference list

Csikszentmihalyi, M. 2008. *Flow: The Psychology of Optimal Experience*. New York: Harper Perennial Modern Classics.

Fischer, P. et al. 2011. 'The Ancestor Effect: Thinking about Our Genetic Origin Enhances Intellectual Performance'. *European Journal of Social Psychology* Vol. 41 No. 1, pp. 11–16.

Siegel, D. 2010. *Mindsight: The New Science of Personal Transformation*. New York: Bantam Books.

Smalley, A. 2013. *Developing the Mindset of a Black Belt*. Sydney: Xlibris.

Dr Weil 2016. 4-7-8 breathing (drweil.com/drw/VDR00160/Dr-Weils. Breathing-Exercise-4-7-8-Breath.html).

6 Embracing mistakes through curiosity

The real voyage of discovery consists not in seeking new lands but in having new eyes.

Marcel Proust

Introduction for teachers and health professionals

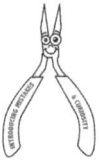

Making mistakes is a natural part of trying new things. Before a skill can build, there must be a starting point – a curiosity to give something a go. Most of the time this curiosity leads to trial and error, and mastery comes with practice and a willingness to learn and build from what went wrong along the way.

For many people, mistakes are perceived as embarrassing failures or a sign that they are not capable. Once they make a mistake they find it hard to get up and try again. They might even try to hide their difficulties because making mistakes brings them a sense of shame. Making mistakes is unavoidable. Some mistakes are bigger than others but all mistakes are a start to learning something new.

Developing curiosity in young people can help nurture a response to mistakes where instead of focusing on what went wrong, you develop a curiosity about what happened, what can be learnt and what can be done differently. Curiosity opens up a positive attitude to uncertainty and error. Rather than seeing these things as cause for anxiety or embarrassment, seeking to understand through curiosity can actually bring pleasure (Kashdan, 2009).

A person with curiosity has a lively interest to know as much as possible about something. When you're curious, things are often more interesting and you notice a broader range of detail. You observe through questions and wonder instead of accepting the world and people as they initially appear.

Children navigate through the world with curiosity, where everything is fresh and novel. Think of a 4-year-old: they're such brilliant advocates for curiosity. New information is often followed with, 'what', 'why?' and 'how?'

Their eagerness to learn and understand how everything works drives them through an enormous learning period. 'What', 'why' and 'how' are three of the most important questions to open up deeper understanding and knowledge about all things. Creativity and open-mindedness spring this level of curiosity.

Sometimes curiosity can take a back seat the older children get. Fostering an environment where young people are continually asking questions creates new connections in their brain, developing a deeper understanding that is more active and engaging. There's an added bonus: curiosity can lead you towards unfamiliar experiences, to take you out of your comfort zone. There's a real buzz that comes from mastering new things and thinking outside the box. When people feel they are capable of rising to challenges and trying new ways of doing things, their wellbeing and resilience strengthen.

Perhaps curiosity's greatest gift is that it contributes to healthier relationships (Kashdan et al., 2011). Curiosity encourages an attitude of openness and genuine interest in others. When people look at each other with curiosity and openness, they are less likely to become bored with them or waste time finding fault and emphasising difference. Mistakes are inevitable in friendships and relationships with others, so embracing mistakes through this kind of curiosity can strengthen these connections.

Explanation for all students

Every time you make a mistake, give yourself a pat on the back. Making mistakes means you are giving things a go. You are trying things out of your comfort zone and giving your brain the exercise it wants and needs. Most new skills and ideas start with mistakes.

A great way to learn from your mistakes is to become curious about them. When you're curious you can discover things that you never knew existed. Instead of getting caught up in your disappointment or embarrassment, next time you make a mistake, start asking questions. Ask yourself questions about what went wrong, why things happened the way they did and, most importantly, what you can learn from and use in the future.

Someone who used curiosity:

Efren Peñaflorida Jr.: CNN Hero of the Year 2009

Efren grew up in an impoverished neighbourhood near a cemetery and a dumpsite. Every night he watched families who didn't have a roof over their heads go to sleep in vacant tombs and every night he went to bed with the smell of rubbish all around him. Efren's hard work and intelligence won him a World Vision scholarship that allowed him to finish school even though his parents had very little money.

On the way to and from school most days, Efren was bullied by gangs of teenagers, who tried to tempt him into a fight. Every day he walked on in silence and never retaliated but inside he felt the pain of their taunts. When Efren was 16 he was approached by the founder of Club 8586 which ran outreach services in the neighbourhood. When Efren was asked if he would volunteer and help the youth on the street, Efren shook his head in frustration and refused. Why should he help out with the people who bullied him for so many years? Efren felt soon after this was a **mistake** and decided to find out more through his **curiosity** about what the club did and why they did it. Efren saw that all people have a story to explain where they are and he believed the young people who taunted him did so because of their own pain and frustration about their difficult lives. He also felt perhaps they lacked mentors to keep them focused on goals, and teachers who would understand them and guide them. Efren began to volunteer for them and, in return, Club 8586 supported him through his secondary and tertiary education.

His **curiosity** about how he could get youth in gangs interested in education was sparked. He founded the Dynamic Teen Company with friends from Club 8586 with the goal of helping youth put their time and energy towards useful things rather than getting involved in drugs and gang wars. Ten years later he and his friends began a pushcart classroom, teaching literacy and values, providing minor health care, healthy snacks and plenty of books and educational toys. Over 10,000 members now work in pushcart classrooms, taking education to the impoverished children and teenagers in the most disadvantaged neighbourhoods in the world.

GROUP DISCUSSION AND BRAINSTORM

Core concept: mistakes

What was the mistake or judgement that Efren made?
Are mistakes a sign of weakness?
What kind of mistakes do people make every day?
Can you think of a time you learnt something because you made a mistake?
What makes it hard to learn from mistakes?
What makes it easier to learn from mistakes?

Being curious when you make a mistake

A short conversation with your students . . .

Everyone who has the courage to try new things will make mistakes along the way. Unless you are a carefully programmed robot you will not get things right all the time or even most of the time! Some mistakes are big and embarrassing and others are small but have an impact on you. One way to learn from mistakes and to cope with them is to be **curious**. That means you ask questions about the 'what', 'how' and 'why' of what happened. You try to know and understand as much as you can about it.

What can make mistakes really hard to handle is judging yourself or others when you or they make a mistake. That means instead of trying to understand what happened you make your mind up based on your own ideas and beliefs. This often means putting yourself or others into categories which aren't very helpful, like 'good or bad' and 'smart or dumb'.

Next time you make a mistake, try and be curious and learn from it.

Sounds like being curious . . . sounds like judging quiz

It's quiz time. Offer the students the statements below and ask them to nod if they think the person is being curious and to shake their head if they are judging.

Quiz statements

CURIOUS = Asking questions to find out more

JUDGING = Putting whatever happened into 'good' or 'bad' type categories without trying to understand why something is the way it is

- That kitten is making such a mess? It must still be learning how to drink milk from a bowl.
- That kitten is so messy.
- What's going wrong for our football team this week? They are slipping all over the playing field! Could it be the rain they're not used to?
- Our football team is not trying hard enough.
- What will help our plants grow better?
- The plants we bought are bad quality.
- She always fights.
- I wonder why she gets into so many fights?
- I don't like him.
- Why don't I understand him yet?
- Mum and dad are being mean.
- I wonder why mum and dad won't let me do that.
- My school lunch tastes boring.
- I wonder why mum packs this in my lunch box.
- It's not fair I lost the race.
- I wonder what I need to do to have a better chance at winning a race.
- I don't like that show everyone in my class likes – it's boring!
- I wonder what everyone in my class likes about that TV show.

Curiosity vs judgement debates

Divide the class into four groups, two curious and two judging. Two groups will be curious when solving the problem and two groups will be judgemental when solving the problem. Divide the problems equally among the groups. Allow a few minutes for each group to come up with a solution based on which perspective they've been asked to take. Once students have prepared their notes, allow them to have a debate based on using curious or judgemental thinking. You can set up chairs in front of each other with room for an audience. Each group takes turns to try and solve the problem using curiosity or judgement. Allow this to flow into a conversation and encourage active listening and turn taking.

Problems for debate

A friendly visiting teacher can't seem to get the class to like him.

A famous home builder has built his two-hundredth house. When the building supervisor comes to inspect the house he is not happy with it.

A group of friends who have always got along with each other are suddenly not talking to each other anymore.

A sports team who have won every game in the season are now losing one game after another – by a lot.

'Best mistake ever' worksheet

Hand out the 'Best mistake ever' worksheet found at the end of this chapter. This worksheet can be used as a one-off to show the importance of mistakes, or more regularly for students who are learning to cope with and forgive themselves for mistakes.

Mistake of the day

Talking about the highs and lows of the day is a great way to connect within a group and share experiences and support each other. This practice has been shown to strengthen relationships, especially when young people are taught to show joy for the other person when they share a positive event (Lambert et al., 2012).

To normalise making mistakes, one way to emphasise the value of them is to add opportunities to share mistakes. At the end of each day you can ask if anyone has a mistake they would like to share. This can encourage discussion about what was learnt from the mistake as well as reassuring the remainder of the group that they are not the only ones making mistakes. The key here is to focus on the learning that follows mistakes. Model and encourage showing empathy as well, to keep everyone feeling connected.

Opening our eyes to curiosity: how much can I find out about one thing? Journal activity

Spark curiosity by letting your students choose something in their classroom they think is interesting. It could be a classroom pet, a poster, an object or an insect. Ask your students to write the object of their choice in their journal and to record answers to your guiding questions. Younger students can draw pictures in response to your questions.

Guiding questions

Does it fit into a category/group?

Where did it come from?

How did it get there?

Does it think? If it thinks, what might it be thinking?

Would all people like it? Why? Why not?

What job does it play in the world?

What place does it have in your life?

Ask your students if they noticed more about their chosen object than they ever have before. Do they have any ideas about what being curious could mean when you're learning, playing and making friends?

Role plays: learning from mistakes

Allow students some time to practise the role plays below and if time permits allow students to showcase their efforts to the group.

You just took a maths test that you worked hard to prepare for last night. The test was much harder than you thought it would be and there were a lot of things you didn't expect in it. Your teacher returns the test later that day and you made more mistakes than correct answers. Show what might have caused this, using curiosity, and show what you have learnt for next time.

You are in a huge rush and you don't want to miss the bus. You grab all your belongings and throw whatever you can into your school bag without doing up the zipper and carry the rest in your arms. As you enter the bus, you trip on the step and everything falls out of your hands. As you bend down to pick it up, the rest of your things fall out of your bag. You feel embarrassed and frustrated and never want this to happen again. Why might this have happened? What have you learnt?

You are really mad at your best friend for something. You start telling another friend how mean your best friend is. They hear you. You feel terrible and know immediately what you have done was a big mistake. Why might you have acted the way you did? What did you learn?

You arrive home and realise you have left your homework book and diary at school. You want to get your homework done and solve this without asking your parents for help. What could you do and learn?

You have been working on a history project and really enjoying it. You arrive at school and the teacher asks the class to hand their projects in. You are shocked. You had it in your diary for next week. How might this have happened? What have you learnt?

You take the last chocolate biscuit from the classroom jar when no one is looking. They are kept as rewards for hard work and reaching goals. The teacher asks you if you took it and you tell a lie and say, 'no'. The minute you say this, you regret it and you want to make it better. Why might you have lied? What have you learnt?

You are responsible for packing your lunchbox and hat into your bag each morning before school. You arrive at school and realise you have left them both at home. This is the second time this has happened this week. You have nothing to eat and won't be allowed to play outside during breaks. How might this have happened? What have you learnt? What can you do to deal with this situation?

You get home and you have left your lunchbox and drink bottle behind at school – again. Your parents are annoyed and you are frustrated with yourself. Why does this keep happening? What can you learn?

Hobbies

Curiosity is at the core of many passions and hobbies. Interest leads to questions and a desire to know as much as possible about the chosen topic. Allow your students some time to discuss in small groups any hobbies or special interests they might have. Once each group has compiled a list of hobbies and interests, record them on a whiteboard.

Hobby challenge

Ask students to choose two hobbies that can easily be tried out at home (without much cost, if any). The first hobby can be one they are interested in and the other one they have no interest in at all. Set a challenge for students to give each hobby a test run during the weeks ahead, engaging in both with curiosity. Allow some journal time for students to record their experience, and later discuss it as a group. Many new passions are ignited through this exercise!

Curiosity in friendships

A short discussion with your students . . .

Friendships are easier when you understand and accept that there are a variety of personality types. Differences between people are more likely to create strength rather than weakness. Being around different ideas and opinions can make you smarter and so does problem solving when those differences generate conflict. Even your favourite people may sometimes annoy and frustrate you. Whenever this happens try and look at the situation with curiosity and find out as much as you can to help you learn and grow from the situation.

Curiosity in friendship challenge

Ask students to think of one person (without naming them) they have had difficulty understanding. Putting aside what they don't like about the person, they can instead ask questions like:

I wonder why they say what they say?
I wonder why they do what they do?
I wonder what they are thinking right now?
I wonder what makes them happy?
I wonder what makes them sad?

Challenge the students to get curious next time they are in a situation where they have differences with the other person. Encourage them to notice how different curiosity feels compared to being angry or annoyed. This is also a great way to approach conflicts between personalities within classrooms.

Curious chatterboxes

Children often enjoy making and playing with paper chatterboxes. Place topics from the list below in a jar. Ask students to pick a topic from the jar. Once they have chosen their topic they need to spend some time either in class or at home researching and being curious about it. When they have gathered enough information they can fill the centre of the chatterbox with 'did you know?' fascinating facts about that topic. This is a fun way to build curiosity in the student making the chatterbox as well as in their peers who get to open it!

Chatterbox topics to get you started

Music   Surfing   Sport   Books   Gardening   TV
Pop stars   Movie stars   Psychology   Astronomy
Astrology   Lego ®   The Olympic Games   Cooking
Volcanoes   Planes   Jokes   Dinosaurs   Kangaroos
The Eiffel Tower   Rock climbing   Ireland   Elephants
Camping   Sharks   Photography   Religion/Spirituality
History   Art   Knights   Chocolate   Insects

Rubber bands

Hand your students two rubber bands each. As you hold the rubber bands up, ask, 'Why were rubber bands invented . . . I wonder who invented them?' Then, leaving them with those questions afloat in their minds, let them know they have ten minutes to find as many uses for the rubber bands as possible. You might let your students go outside the classroom or remain indoors. Let their curiosity delve into the properties of a rubber band and see what further questions arise once students have shared their inventions. Younger students will need guidance about safety when using rubber bands.

What's in the box?

Choose an interesting item and place it inside a box. (You could even padlock the box to create more excitement and curiosity!) Let the students know you have placed something interesting in there. Let them know the box will remain closed/locked until someone guesses its contents. Leave 24 hours before any guesses can be submitted to keep your students thinking, and only allow one guess per person per day. This really puts the pressure on everyone to show curiosity and to think creatively instead of blurting answers out on impulse.

The person to guess the contents can have the contents! Some teachers keep this activity going throughout the year, refilling the box over and over to keep those curious minds working. For younger students it can help to offer a theme (e.g. 'I am found underground' for a crystal) so they know roughly what area the special object is from.

Possible items: silly putty, magnifying glass, crystals, fossils, fancy erasers, IOU a class party voucher, free play voucher, DVD, chocolate, seeds, fidget toys, a coin from overseas . . .

Kitchen chemistry

Scientific experiments are a great way to ignite curiosity and explore mistakes. Most schools will have plenty of books with scientific experiments, or they can be found online to suit you. Demonstrate an interesting experiment or allow everyone to have a go. Introduce the experiment with enthusiasm and curiosity. Ask questions like, 'I wonder what is about to happen?' Once you have demonstrated the reaction, ask, 'I wonder why that happened?' Allow the class the rest of the day to consider it, and ask them to return in the morning with their best answer. Allow time to ponder, question and build curiosity. If you are lucky enough to have an experiment not turn out as planned, enjoy brainstorming together as a group about what the mistake might have been. You may also like to cause a mistake on purpose and allow the group to problem solve together.

Weekly challenge

Set a goal for students to find out as much about one topic as they can over the period of a week. The catch is, they are not allowed to use the internet! They need to ask as many questions as they can of themselves and others and use what they have learned about curious thinking. Allow them to put together a short talk or movie presentation titled, 'Ten Things I Never Knew About . . .'. The idea is to test ideas out, check out what other people know, and research through books. As convenient as a Google search is, it dulls opportunities for curiosity as the answers come too easily. People actually enjoy wondering what the answer is to something more than finding out the answer; so delaying gratification is well worth it for a good burst of dopamine.

Parent tips for building curiosity and learning through mistakes

Try to be curious

We are all born curious, but over time we may lose this sense of excitement at discovering something new and wanting to know more about it. Fostering your own curiosity and modelling this to your children is an important step in building curious minds.

Encourage exploration

When your child is learning and exploring something new, try not to interrupt them with your own concerns. Resist the urge to interrupt what they are doing if you feel they need guidance as this can stop your child from tuning into their own instincts about what they are doing. It can also make them too reliant on you as a compass for what they should and shouldn't try. Too many 'don'ts' and 'be carefuls' can squash their curiosity and enthusiasm for exploration. While there is always a place for 'don't' and 'be careful', most of the time getting a little dirty is the beginning of curiosity and is followed by great learning and joy.

Learning from mistakes

While it may be tempting to protect children from unnecessary disappointment, learning how to handle life's ups and downs with confidence comes through experience and practice. Allowing your children to make mistakes, to come last, to hand in something late because they didn't organise their time, gives them important experiences which build emotional resilience. Avoiding these learning opportunities in childhood makes them even more difficult to deal with in the teenage years and into early adulthood.

If a child only experiences success and avoids tasks they don't excel at, eventually this catches up with them. When your child is struggling with an assignment and their work is looking less than acceptable, encourage your child but avoid polishing their efforts for them. Giving them the answers, or doing some of it for them, ultimately takes away a learning opportunity to receive constructive feedback from their teacher.

Create a space for disappointment

When your child is disappointed or when they have made a mistake, try showing empathy, not solutions. Often when a child is feeling a strong emotion like disappointment the temptation is to rescue them from the feeling. Using distraction, diversion and a promise of it being better next time all suggest there is something wrong with having the feeling. Instead, acknowledge your child's feelings by labelling them and kindly letting them know, 'You look so disappointed. I'm here for you.' Not much more needs to be said. There is no need to wish them better luck next time or make an excuse for why they didn't come out on top this time. Doing this makes them feel that disappointment and other strong emotions need to be fixed, excused or ignored.

Celebrate mistakes

Curiosity often leads to mistakes. This is a good thing. Every time your child 'fails' and has another go they are showing determination and persistence and building a natural curiosity to learn. Celebrate it by asking your children at dinner on some nights, 'what was your biggest mistake today?' Listen with interest and enthusiasm and see where the conversation might lead. When you notice your child bouncing back from a mistake make sure you acknowledge it with pride.

Model a love of learning

Show your children you are a lifelong learner and always willing to try something new. If you don't know the answer to something, avoid the 'I don't know' or 'ask your father/mother' response and instead say, 'I don't know but I am going to find out!' Learn new skills yourself or as a family to show you are curious and interested in new things even if they are unfamiliar and you haven't yet got the skills to do them.

Model an acceptance of mistakes

When you make a mistake try and embrace it – even have a laugh about it. Use the word 'mistake' freely around your children and show you are okay with feeling vulnerable and not getting everything right all the time. Let your children tell you what you could have done differently and ask them for inspiration and motivation when you are struggling to get the hang of something. When you have made a mistake and learned an interesting lesson, tell your children about it with just as much enthusiasm as you would tell them about something you succeeded in!

Embrace change

Embrace change in small steps – for example, swapping where everyone sits at the dinner table, moving furniture around occasionally, or even eating breakfast cereal for dinner one night! Engage in conversations about the nature of change and how it is a natural part of life. Talk about the opportunities that might come with change, using questions like, 'What would happen if the seasons never changed' or 'What if you stayed the same size you were when you were born?' and see what conversations come up.

Seek answers

Ask your children, 'why?' as much as possible to show your own curiosity about what they're talking about. Teach them to look for information and do this together when you can. When you do know the answer to something, instead of giving it to them freely, try asking, 'What do you think the answer could be?' Show confidence in your child to work it out.

Go on adventures

Exploring new places outdoors is a gateway for curiosity. Be sure to ask questions like, 'I wonder what lives in that tree?', 'I wonder where that path leads to?', 'I wonder what that bird call means to the bird that's listening?', 'I wonder why that tree is shaped like that?' and so forth. Try not to call out everything you see that is interesting. Instead you can say, 'There is something really interesting up ahead. I wonder if you can work out what I am looking at?'

Try geocaching

Geocaching is gaining interest in neighbourhoods around the world. This outdoor 'treasure hunt' is a great way to build curiosity and exploration in children of all ages. Most cities have geocaching websites where you can download the App and create a geocaching account to help you go on treasure hunts all over the world!

BEST MISTAKE EVER

Congratulations! You made a mistake. Making a mistake means you are showing courage to learn something new and you are challenging yourself. Whenever you make a mistake try and learn something from it.
Being curious about why some things worked and why some things didn't work helps you learn from the mistake.

'Anyone who has never made a mistake has never tried anything new.' **(Albert Einstein)**

What was the mistake you made?
Write and draw about it here

What did you learn from the mistake?
Write and draw about it here

QUESTIONS TO ASK YOUNG PEOPLE TO ENCOURAGE SELF-AWARENESS AND HELP STUDENTS LEARN FROM MISTAKES

Self-judgement questions

How are you going with this challenge?
How do you think you went with the test?
What do you think of your work?
Do you like what you have done?
What do you like about it?
What don't you like about it? (If anything.)
Did you find it challenging?
Did you find it easy?

Self-improvement questions

Could you have done anything differently?
What could you have done more/less of to find this easier/more interesting?
What could have made it easier/more interesting?
What could I have done as your teacher/mentor to help you more with this task?

Self-monitoring questions

Did you enjoy it?
Did you give it your best effort?
Do you think you stayed with the challenge even when it was tough?
What helped you persist?
What got in the way of persisting?
What part did you enjoy?
What part didn't you enjoy?
Were you surprised at how things turned out?
Would you like to try something like this again?

Reference list

Kashdan, T. 2009. *Curious? Discover the Missing Ingredient to a Fulfilling Life*. New York: HarperCollins.

Kashdan, T. et al. 2011. 'When Curiosity Breeds Intimacy: Taking Advantage of Intimacy Opportunities and Transforming Boring Conversations'. *Journal of Personality* Vol. 79, pp. 1369–1401.

Lambert, N. M. et al. 2012. 'A Boost of Positive Affect: The Perks of Sharing Positive Experiences'. *Journal of Social and Personal Relationships* Vol. 30, pp. 24–43.

7 Persistence and the value of hard work

Character consists of what you do on the third and fourth tries.

James A. Michener

Introduction for teachers and health professionals

Persistence is the strength and determination to hang in a little longer when times are tough. Most things would be easier if persistence were easier! Persistence is by nature very challenging and it would help if more young people knew this. Instead, many students think some people are just naturally more persistent than others. What they don't see is that even the most persistent person still finds persisting tough!

When anyone 'gives up' it is usually because the task has become too difficult, or they became distracted, or they lost their motivation, or all of the above. We can all relate to these obstacles. Think of the last time you made a pact with yourself to change a habit. Let's say it was to eat less chocolate. You were doing just fine until you walked past the chocolate shop. There it was in front of you. The fruit shop was right across from where you stood and although you could satisfy your 'hunger' for something sweet with a punnet of delicious blueberries, your eyes returned to the chocolate. You made eye contact with the sales person and there – it's all over! You made your purchase. Persisting was difficult, the chocolate distracted you and your motivation to eat fruit instead went out the window!

Similar distractions occur when you learn something new and challenging. Feelings of frustration are part of the experience as obstacles confront you along your way. Inevitably, there will be moments where you want to give up and do something else. To reach new levels of understanding, however, you have to push through those challenges. Few things come easily and the things that do rarely give you the buzz you get from that 'eureka' moment that follows persistent hard work.

Pride and a sense of accomplishment usually follow, reinforcing those who persist to try more and more things. When students know that the feel-good pay-off from persistence only comes after less comfortable feelings like frustration they are keener to keep going and are less likely to think they're incapable just because they found something difficult. It is perfectly normal to find new challenges difficult and mastery takes time, problem solving and practice.

Grit and persistence

While persistence might be one of the hardest things to build for many young people, it is one of the highest-ranking predictors of overall student achievement. Duckworth (2016) defines persistence as, 'Grit: The tendency to sustain interest in and effort toward very long-term goals.' She has demonstrated that people who sustain effort and show 'grit' in learning have better academic outcomes than others with higher IQs. Research into building 'grit' is still very much in its infancy but educators and health professionals alike agree on its importance.

The growth mindset and persistence

Professor Carol Dweck's work on the growth mindset has led the way to encourage the development of persistence – or grit. Dweck (2012) has identified two mindsets when people are learning. The *growth mindset* sees intelligence and ability as constantly developing rather than fixed. Within a growth mindset the focus is on effort and the process of learning. People with a growth mindset do not see mistakes as permanent or as failures. They see them as opportunities to learn and grow. On the other hand, a *fixed mindset* gets lost in the *now* of learning and when the person feels challenged or makes a mistake they interpret it as a lack of intelligence and tend to give up quickly. The fixed mindset focuses on outcomes without relating this to the effort and persistence behind those outcomes.

Motivation and persistence

Understanding the nature of persistence is a beginning point, but to keep persisting, motivation is essential. For some, it is enough to think about and imagine themselves reaching their goal. Their belief in their ability to achieve the goal might be high and this might be enough to keep them motivated. Encouragement from mentors and family helps keep people motivated, as well as being recognised for their efforts towards a goal. Sometimes motivation needs to come from other sources as well. A motivation survey is offered later to help students identify what motivates them.

This chapter teaches young people about the nature of persistence, the value of hard work and effort, and the importance of motivation and self-assessment.

Persistence explained (for younger students)

Persistence is when you keep trying even when things get tough. When things around you look easier and more fun you try and ignore them and stay focused on what you are working on. When you persist you are brave enough to handle the big feelings that everyone gets when they learn something new and difficult. Persistent people know that getting frustrated is part of learning, and learning new things is not always easy. Once you learn something new, you feel happy and proud. Learning new things takes time, hard work and practice. The more you persist, the stronger your brain will get at persisting!

Persistence explained (for older students)

Persistence is when you keep going with something even when it gets tough. Even the most persistent people don't find persistence easy. Sticking with something that's hard work isn't easy and people usually have moments of real frustration when learning gets hard. Persistent people know tough times don't last and if you take them on as a challenge with determination you're going to get through them!

To persist you often have to resist other temptations around you, like fun and easier things. When you're persistent you stay focused on your goal. When you show courage through the tough feelings like frustration and exhaustion you are rewarded with pride and happiness that you have mastered something new. Your brain gets stronger the more you practise persistence.

Someone who used persistence and hard work:

Thandiwe Chama: International Children's Peace Prize awardee 2007, aged 16

When Thandiwe was 8, her school in Zambia suddenly closed down. She knew going to school was her best chance of having a better life and being able to take care of herself. Thandiwe stood up that day and led a group of sixty children in a long and exhausting walk, determined to find another school. From that day on, Thandiwe became an educational rights activist and has been a big part of developing Zambia's education system. She works hard, with a persistent message that all children have a right to an education no matter what. There are a lot more schools and opportunities for education in Zambia today because of her hard work. When she was 16 she won the International Children's Peace Prize award for her blog, titled 'CRC' (Children's Rights Club). She has also opened her own library, 'Thandiwe's Library', for children in Zambia from all walks of life. Thandiwe believes the more people she helps to access education and the more children know that they too have rights, the more young people will grow up to contribute to their communities, making the world a better and fairer place.

GROUP DISCUSSION AND BRAINSTORM: How does persistence feel?

Divide the class into small groups and begin a brainstorm about what it feels like to learn something new and difficult. The central concept is 'persistence'. Younger students can do this activity as a whole class rather than in small groups.

Return the group together and allow each group to share their comments. Acknowledge persistence is one of the most challenging skills they will ever develop but also one of the most useful for reaching their potential.

BRAINSTORM

Central concept: working hard

What does it mean to work hard?

Is the feeling that you're working hard on something a sign you are not capable?

Is it possible to achieve as much with less effort (less hard work)?

When does working hard pay off?

When doesn't working hard pay off?

'Mountains of persistence' guide sheet

Hand out the 'Mountains of persistence' guide sheet found at the end of this chapter. Ask your students if they can think of ways to link persistence to climbing a mountain. Extend the discussion by encouraging students to notice what kinds of thoughts and feelings come in and out of your mind while you're persisting.

'Persistence challenge' worksheet

Hand out the 'Persistence challenge' worksheet found at the end of this chapter. Explain to students their goal is to think of an area where they would benefit from being more persistent. Add that there will be a part of the worksheet that requires them to assess themselves on their efforts. Teaching young people self-assessment contributes to their overall learning outcomes (Hattie, 2008).

Motivation

A short conversation with your students . . .

When you are setting goals or trying something new, you need motivation. Motivation is a feeling inside you that you want to reach your goal or learn something new. It makes you feel energetic and even excited. Sometimes you will feel motivated by what happens after you reach your goal or learn something new. For example, you might want to learn to swim. What motivates you might be that you will be able to go to pool parties without wearing floaties. Or, the feeling of confidence you get from being able to swim better might motivate you.

Motivation survey

Hand out the motivation survey at the end of this chapter to help students work out what might motivate them to persist towards reaching their goals and trying new things. They can add their motivators to their goal setting worksheets as a reminder as well.

Role plays

Offer the following role plays in pairs or small groups to tackle practical ways to work hard and persist – even when it gets tough. Try and encourage students to show their thinking, feeling, planning and self-encouragement strategies. They can also add a motivational aspect to show what kept them persistent.

ROLE PLAY

You really want to be in the school play. You especially would like to get the lead part. You love acting but when you perform in front of other people it takes you some time to warm up and feel confident. Once you get started you can really rock the stage! It is getting close to audition time. You know all the lines but whenever you perform to another person you go all wobbly. Sometimes you feel you are not ready for this.

You have been working to build a very complex Lego® set all week. It is designed for people much older than you and it really has been challenging. You are almost finished when your sister knocks it over by accident. You are so mad and you can't begin to imagine how you will rebuild it.

Something you have been saving up for for ages is on sale. That means you only need $10 to get it during the sale, instead of $40. You want it so much. The sale ends in one week and you have two assignments and a test due this week. How will you fit school work and jobs in?

Your teacher talks about a competition that all students in your year level can enter. Whoever is judged to have written the best poem about the environment can go to another state with the principal for a national competition. The prize money is enough to get you the new bike you have been hoping for and you love the idea of travelling in a plane. The thing is, you love writing – just not poems . . .

All your friends are riding skateboards. You have your older sister's one but you are really nervous about going on it. The nerves are getting in the way of you learning how to use it and you are starting to feel left out when your friends talk about skateboarding.

You have lost something very special to you while playing in the park. You spent the whole afternoon at this park and used all areas! You are determined to find it but you are tired and losing hope. What will keep you going?

You really want to prove to your parents you can keep your room tidy every day without their help. They have agreed to get you a new bunk bed once you have proven this for the whole school term. You are finding it really hard to stay organised and keep things tidy even though you are trying your best. How will you persist?

You have often struggled with spelling and it gets in the way of you getting 'A' grades in literacy. You work really hard at spelling every week and nothing seems to improve. You are losing your motivation and you are feeling pretty down about it. What will keep you persisting? Is it time to ask for help? Or not?

One more minute!

Choose an activity for your class that involves working up a sweat. It could be jogging, running laps of the playing field, skipping, push-ups – anything that is quickly tiring. Place students in pairs, then one partner watches the other while holding a stopwatch (make sure both people get a turn to exercise). Explain the challenge here is to do the designated exercise and right at the moment where they feel like they want to give up, they call out to their partner, 'This is tough! I want to stop!' Their partner then presses the stopwatch and says, 'one more minute!' The challenge is for the child to keep persisting for as long as possible – trying to reach that additional minute. This is good hands-on experience for the discomfort discussed in this chapter, which happens when you are struggling with persistence. In exercise, this point of persistence is where strength comes from, and in learning it is where new skills come from. Younger students or less athletically capable groups might need to build up to one minute. Using your judgement adjust the time accordingly. Even 'ten more seconds' can get the message across.

Ice cube challenge

Materials: enough ice cubes to provide one for each student. This activity is best done in the warmer months and outside on grass.

In pairs, each person is given an ice cube. On 'go' all participants place the ice cube on their head. Whoever in the pair keeps it on their head the longest wins. The game can be extended by offering a final round, where all winners of the first round divide again into pairs and this continues until only one pair is left and an ultimate ice cube persistence champion can be celebrated!

Buttery bliss

Materials: small transparent containers such as empty plastic water bottles; whipping cream (enough for all students to half-fill their containers). Optional: pancake batter to make pancakes later to enjoy the butter with.

Younger students are really tested for their persistence with this one and enjoy the energetic nature of the task. Older students have just as much fun with it and enjoy the competition that is often associated with getting to a completed product.

Half-fill the small container with whipping cream. You might wish to do this in advance for younger students and provide funnels to pour the cream in.

Let students know that those who persist long enough will have fresh butter they can take home and use as a spread (or use on pancakes afterwards).

Shaking the container to and fro with a reasonable grasp and speed will eventually turn the cream into butter! Encourage students with sore arms to problem solve (e.g. change hands, take a break, use positive self-talk, 'I will finish this', and so forth). Try not to place all the focus on the finished product and remind the students to enjoy the process of making butter. Play some music, tell some jokes and, when a student appears to be giving up, step in where you can, move closer and give them special encouragement of their own.

Paper clip/pipe cleaner sculptures

Materials: enough paper clips for each pair to have twenty.

Divide the class into pairs. Provide each pair with paper clips. Allow them an opportunity to discuss as a pair what they plan to 'sculpt' within the time limit of 5–10 minutes. The completed sculpture must combine both partners' ideas and will be free-standing using as many paper clips as possible. Themes make the task more challenging and interesting – for example, sculptures must be of something starting with the letter 'S', or all sculptures must represent something the partners have in common. Younger students might work better alone, or instead of paper clips try pipe cleaners, which are easier for small hands to manipulate.

Card towers

Materials: several packs of playing cards.

This activity can be done individually, in pairs or in larger groups. The task is straightforward but challenging enough that it will require persistence – especially when the cards fall or things don't go according to plan. Aim for students to build towers using as many cards as in the pack with the goal of making it as *interesting* as possible. Often young people go for *biggest* or *tallest*, whereas focusing on interest opens up creativity and reduces competition amongst students. Other variations of this activity include building a famous landmark (e.g. the Eiffel Tower), or building card 'buildings' towards the centre of the room with the goal for them to all connect into one 'building'.

Knots galore!

Materials: enough 30 cm strips of thin to medium rope for students to practise tying knots. These can be purchased from craft and fabric stores. Scarves from home can also be used as an alternative.

Learning to tie knots can be very challenging – as can untying them! (This activity can be even more challenging when you ask students to do the knots blindfolded once they have mastered the initial skill.)

There are plenty of knotting and folding projects you can try at the following sites:

www.animatedknots.com
www.animatednapkins.com

Human chain

Divide the class into lines consisting of approximately five students. The person in front puts their left hand under their legs and grabs the right hand of the person behind them. They continue to make this link until everyone in their line is connected. Once each team has a human chain, allow them to take a walk around the space, challenging them to stay linked together. When the chain becomes undone, the group is challenged to correct their chain. Depending on the group and time available you might also wish to allow the 'chains' to race each other.

Rubber band cork/block challenge

Materials: one bottle cork or building block for each pair; plenty of rubber bands of various sizes.

Divide the class into pairs and provide each pair with one block or cork each. Hand out a variety of rubber bands with different colours, lengths and widths, which adds to the challenge. Set the timer for one minute (or longer), during which each person must wrap the rubber bands around their partner's block/cork. Some can be tightly bound around and others purposefully placed loosely. You can allow one to two minutes depending on the age and abilities of the group. On 'go' students exchange blocks/corks and try to unravel the rubber bands their partner has bound for them without tangling or snapping them.

Origami

Materials: plenty of plain or patterned origami/craft paper – paper must be cut into squares.

Origami and other types of paper craft provide lots of opportunities for trial and error and often require plenty of persistence. Online video clips are readily available for children to easily follow the steps to fold an origami figure. Check the various sites first to ensure the project is challenging but within your students' reach (often the best way to do this is to try folding it yourself). With the technology of a smart board, you should be able to show a folding sequence to your students easily and you might learn it for the first time with them. This way you can show how you handle the challenge, vocalising and modelling persistence.

Class puzzle

Place a jigsaw puzzle on a table pitched at slightly above your class's general ability. The puzzle can be worked on casually by all members of the class, or small groups can tackle it together in structured breaks. Puzzles are a wonderful way to practise persistence and problem solving over a period of time. Photographing your students at the various stages of solving the puzzle through to completion can provide an excellent foundation for a persistence poster.

Weekly challenge

Allow students a few minutes to think of something they find challenging at home and another thing they find challenging at school. Using the 'Persistence challenge' worksheet at the end of the chapter, guide students to break tasks down into daily steps rather than making one statement of what they are trying to do.

For example, instead of saying they will learn their times tables by the end of the week, they could aim to learn three tables a day. This encourages regular self-assessment and feedback from you, increasing motivation and a sense of achievement. Younger students might need help completing the worksheet and will need reminders from an adult to attempt each daily challenge. They could do drawings of what they will achieve instead of writing. It is never too early to teach young people to organise their goals and break them down into manageable components.

Inspiration: if your students struggle to find an area to challenge themselves in, consider the list below:

Younger children: riding a bike without trainer wheels, learning to write their own name, separating from parents with courage, asking for help in class, learning ball skills, learning to roller skate, sports, being organised, and so forth.

Older children: sports, being more organised, learning times tables, eating healthier food, getting to bed earlier, learning a language, learning an instrument, learning to roller skate, and so forth.

Parent tips

Focus on the process not the product, their efforts not the outcome

From as early as possible show your children that you are interested in the way they are learning, rather than how much they are learning. Comment on their approach to an activity and what they are doing as the activity unfolds. Pay less attention to the final product. For example, if your child is building something, you might say, 'You look like you're really enjoying yourself' and 'That looks tough – is it tough?' and 'I wonder what you will do next.' Let them know you have noticed them working hard and trying their best. Focus more on their effort and hard work instead of whether or not you think the project was of a high standard.

Encourage rather than praise

Everyone grows from encouragement. Knowing someone not only believes in you but also wants to be part of coaching and mentoring you gives courage.

Praise usually leaves children wanting more and becoming 'hooked' on hearing how well they are doing. When you have been praised excessively you seek praise and feedback from others to gauge how you are doing. Encouragement on the other hand offers support and guidance but asks you to assess for yourself how you are doing. See below for a comparison between encouragement and praise:

Child reaches the next level in swimming
Praise: You are a swimming champion!
Encouragement: You worked hard at this. You've really earned that next level.

Child draws a picture and asks for your opinion
Praise: It's beautiful!
Encouragement: You look like you really enjoyed yourself. What do you think of it?

Child wins in a race
Praise: You are the fastest runner I've ever seen!
Encouragement: Running is one of your strengths. Did you have fun?

Teenager gets their driving licence
Praise: I knew you'd get it.
Encouragement: You did everything you could to practise enough and earn this. Well done.

Teenager gets invited to a big party
Praise: You're so popular.
Encouragement: It is great to see you've made some new friends.

Teenager wins a school drama prize
Praise: You are the best actor in the school.
Encouragement: You must feel so proud after all the time you put into the play.

Teach your child self-assessment

Young people often grow up looking to their parents and others to tell them how they are doing. After finishing a drawing, the pattern is usually to run up to someone and show them their completed work. While it is always useful to encourage, it is also important to ask young people what they think of their work as well. Carefully balance your encouragement with questions such as, 'What do you think of it?', 'Do you like it?', 'What do you like most about it?' and 'Was it hard/easy/fun?' You can also add comments like, 'You look like you had fun!', 'You look really happy with what you've drawn!', 'You used your favourite blue all through it!' This way you are focusing on their efforts and the process involved rather than labelling it with little meaning.

Give regular feedback on effort and hard work

Sometimes it is easy to focus on completed tasks and end products. When we do this, the focus is removed from the planning, problem solving and effort going into most tasks. Young people become too focused on outcomes and perfection, hoping to receive another dose of praise to keep them feeling motivated. Try noticing your child's effort in what they do and congratulate them for working hard. When they don't come first or do as well as expected in something, pay attention to the effort they put in.

Talk about the difficult feelings associated with effort and persistence

When your child is ready to give up or is struggling, empathise. You might say, 'It's tough isn't it?', acknowledging you have noticed their experience. When you are struggling with persistence, talk through your feelings so they can see you also find persistence challenging.

Challenge yourself or the family to learn a new skill together

Depending on your children's ages, choose an activity you can all learn together. Begin by having a discussion about what family members have always wanted to learn. Ideas include sewing, knitting, skating, juggling, painting, sculpting, mosaic, singing, playing an instrument, kayaking, orienteering, sports, camping and so on. Select the ones your family can realistically learn together and pick them out of a jar every now and again. Enjoy learning the skill together, encouraging and helping each other while sharing the need for persistence through the challenging times.

Let your child teach you something

Young people are usually the ones being taught and challenged. Allow your children to teach you something they enjoy like words to a favourite song, a magic trick, a silly dance, a language and so forth. Let them help you when you are feeling challenged, and show how well you can persist with it.

Teach your child to compromise

If your child is a little too persistent and finds it hard to let things go when they have an idea in their head, suggest they look for a solution that gives everyone involved something they want. Remind them the other person might have strong ideas and wishes too. Teach them to understand what each person's key need is and then look for a way to resolve the situation accounting for this. This takes persistence and understanding.

Encourage your child to see things through

If your child is quick to quit new activities try finding out more about what might be bothering them. They could need more warm-up time, practice at home or an opportunity to talk about a fear they might have. Do as much as you can to maintain your child's involvement in something new for as long as possible – especially if you see they are in fact enjoying themselves and growing from the experience. Many young people stop doing an activity they would potentially gain benefit from because anxiety, frustration and shyness got in the way. If you feel your child is really struggling, try and maintain the expectation they attend for a set period, such as until the school term ends. Also remember that it is hard to persist if you are over-committed to too many extra-curricular activities. If this might be the case, it is worth reviewing how much your child is doing and whether or not they need to give up an activity or two.

Show persistence

Children learn through observation, especially when watching someone they love and admire. Normalising your challenges and seeing them as opportunities to learn and grow will help your child develop these skills also. If your child observes you feeling bowled over by challenges and abandoning them when things get tough, they too are likely to see this as a way out of the frustration. When you are faced with the inevitable challenges of family and work life, role model a 'can do' attitude and show your children you are doing as much as possible in your power to persist through. It is okay to show you find it challenging as long as you do this with a hopeful, optimistic and solution-focused outlook.

Break tasks down

It can be overwhelming to manage the range of big emotions associated with challenges and persistence. Breaking tasks down into small achievable chunks where regular feedback for efforts can be offered can help support persistence and resilience. Cleaning a room can feel overwhelming for anyone but young people's brains often get lost in the size of the task as well as the temptation to escape to more interesting things! Breaking a task like this down into smaller tasks and providing encouragement along the way can maintain persistence longer.

Show visual representations of tasks

Sometimes persistence becomes overwhelming for young people when they are holding too much information in their head about what needs doing. If you are able to provide them with visual information about the steps involved in persisting through something, clearly marking an end point, this can reduce stress and encourage persistence.

Help your child understand the usefulness of what they are learning

A student who doesn't understand or value learning is unlikely to persist towards academic and creative achievement. Help them understand and develop their strengths and understand why learning can be useful and enjoyable. As often as you can, relate new learning to real life and how it can benefit them. Show the value in learning about history or the usefulness of being able to calculate things in your head. Empathise when some learning seems difficult to place in an 'important' category or is just not interesting! Encourage them to keep going no matter what, and show you have faith they will.

Understand your child's personality

Some personalities and temperaments develop persistence faster. The child with a sunny and resilient temperament is less likely to feel threatened by difficulties in learning something new and will find it easier to persist. The child with anxiety, on the other hand, might react to their body's fight, flight or freeze response and want to escape the situation and give up. Keep this in mind when responding to your child when they are feeling challenged and show empathy and acceptance for who they are. Always maintain confidence in them to reach their potential.

Be patient with young people with learning difficulties

Learners who try as hard as their peers but are slower to learn need special mention here. Day in day out they come to school and put in more effort than is needed by their peers to learn new things. They are the first to show fatigue, early to give up and hold a strong emotional presence in the classroom. How do you keep them persisting? These students need mentoring from others, consistent guidance and encouragement, more manageable and suitable tasks, and rewards for their efforts. Reward systems can help students who struggle to increase their motivation while they develop the necessary skills to achieve more. The motivation to use effort can then become intrinsic as they experience success, a natural motivator to keep going.

MOUNTAINS OF PERSISTENCE

Persisting is when you keep working on something, even when it gets tough.
Persisting is usually hard. The reward is, you proved to yourself you could do it and learnt something new.
Persisting makes your **brain stronger** and your life more **interesting.**

PERSISTENCE CHALLENGE

My Challenge:
_____

How I feel about working on it:
_____
_____
_____
_____

How I will feel when I have mastered it:
_____
_____
_____
_____

Use the table below to record what you will do to work towards your challenge and how you felt after you worked on it. Give yourself a rating out of 5 to show how persistent you were.

	What I did to work on my challenge.	How I felt about what I did. (Circle)	Persistence self-rating out of 5
Day 1		😟 😐 😃	
Day 2		😟 😐 😃	
Day 3		😟 😐 😃	
Day 4		😟 😐 😃	
Day 5		😟 😐 😃	

PERSISTENCE SELF-RATING SCALE
(**1**=didn't try **2**=tried a little **3**=half and half effort **4**=tried most of the time **5**=gave it my very best effort)

MOTIVATION SURVEY

Tick anything that motivates and energises you to work extra hard on a goal. Use these motivators next time you set a goal. Add your own ideas at the end too!

- ☐ Background music.
- ☐ Exercising before working on my goal.
- ☐ Taking short breaks while working on my goal.
- ☐ Feeling grateful for what is going on around me.
- ☐ Affirmations (e.g. 'I can do this', 'I believe anything is possible' and 'I am focused')
- ☐ Testing ideas through experiments and practice.
- ☐ Feeling proud.
- ☐ Being encouraged by others.
- ☐ Reading more about what I am working towards.
- ☐ Research on the internet.
- ☐ Talking to someone about my goals.
- ☐ Aiming for a goal with someone else. (a goal buddy)
- ☐ Celebrations for working hard and reaching goals.
- ☐ Looking forward to doing something fun after my hard work.
- ☐ Creating a movie about my journey towards my goal.
- ☐ Exercising my brain and making it stronger.
- ☐ Special time with someone.

My ideas for motivation

EFFORT SELF-ASSESSMENT

Rate your effort towards any goal out of five here.

Name:_____

My goal: _____
_____
_____

Date started:_____

I will know I have reached my goal when: _____
_____
_____

A person encouraging me with my goal: _____

Day	Self-rating	Self-report on my rating
Mon	/5	....
Tue	/5	....
Wed	/5	....
Thur	/5	....
Fri	/5	....
Sat	/5	....
Sun	/5	....

PERSISTENCE

Self-rating scale:
(**1**=I made no effort on this today **2**=I made some effort but got distracted by other things **3**=I made a pretty good effort but other things kept getting in the way **4**=I tried hard on this most of the time and ignored a lot of distractions **5**=I gave it my very best effort and ignored distractions)

Reference list

Duckworth, A. 2016. *Grit: The Power of Passion and Perseverance*. Sydney: Simon and Schuster.

Dweck, C. 2012. *Mindset: How You Can Fulfil Your Potential*. London: Constable.

Hattie, J. 2008. *Visible Learning for Teachers: Maximizing Impact on Learning*. London: Routledge.

8 Setting goals

There is joy in work. There is no happiness except in the realisation that we have accomplished something.

Henry Ford

An introduction for teachers and health professionals

People set goals all the time – that's the easy part. Most of us know what we *want* to achieve. Whether it's learning to make sushi, eating more healthily or exercising more, *completion of a goal* is often where people get stuck. Setting regular and realistic goals builds resilience. Goals do not necessarily have to be fully realised for this to be true. Resilience comes through learning from goals that were not reached, just as much as from the sense of accomplishment when a task is completed.

Goals don't have to be so big or admirable that people drop to their knees and applaud you for reaching them. In fact, as much as people often seek approval and appreciation, you don't build resilience from other people's approval. You build resilience from your own sense of approval – from feeling capable and taking pride in yourself for your own efforts. Every goal achieved is a reminder that you are capable. Feeling capable energises and motivates. It's a giant tick in your mind that you're on track and using your time effectively. You are on a journey, you have direction, and you are capable.

Goal achievement releases dopamine, a feel-good hormone, further increasing wellbeing. A burst of happiness brings along with it a new lease of energy. It feels good and you want to experience that good feeling again, so you are more likely to set more goals. The more goals you set and achieve, the more dopamine is released and the better your sense of wellbeing becomes. This works in reverse too. If you are not achieving enough goals because they were set too high or are too far into the future, your dopamine levels deplete. You may feel anxious and lose your motivation to persist; your sense of wellbeing and resilience drop (Mehta, 2013).

Teaching young people as early as possible how to set realistic goals provides them with one of the most useful lifelong skills they need. Goals keep your students' focus on the present as well as what they hope to achieve in the future. Each time they experience success through goal completion, their brain stores important information about what helped them through, preparing them for the next challenge. When they do not reach their goals, they need your encouragement and guidance to figure out what worked, what didn't work and what they might have learnt from the process. The best guidance comes through helping a child focus on their efforts and intentions. Add some consistent effort and the occasional dash of good luck and there you have it, a solid contribution towards overall achievement.

Motivating students to set goals

While encouragement is a great place to start, students benefit when the goal is both desirable and within their reach. In other words, if a student thinks the goal is unachievable or not personally motivating, the likelihood of them achieving it, even with hard work, is greatly reduced (Schunk, 1991).

Working towards goals takes a lot of hard work, and hard work is driven by motivation. There are a number of ways to provide your students with the best chance to stay motivated through their goals. The first is making them short-term. Particularly in the early stages of becoming a goal setter, students should aim for relatively short-term goals. Within a week or a couple of weeks is ideal for primary age students, and younger students may have goals to achieve within the hour or day. Most goals set by young people should avoid being further away than a couple of months. (When you're young, two months feels like an eternity! That's too long for a young person to experience the rewards of their efforts.)

Being specific about goals also contributes to motivation. Telling a student to 'learn your five times table' is far less effective than 'aim to learn three times tables a day over four days'. Students also need help understanding their strengths, limits and values. The closer these are matched to their learning and social emotional goals, the more likely they are to show persistence. Striking a balance where students are challenged but capable, and where tasks are short-term and encouraged with regular feedback, increases goal achievement and persistence (Schunk and Zimmerman, 2006).

Finally, goals should challenge your students enough that they need to work hard and problem solve, but not so much that they become overwhelmed. If goals are too easy, motivation will be high at first but will drop in time (Schunk and Zimmerman, 2006). The student will yearn for the buzz of learning something new, feeling challenged and being rewarded from the success that follows hard work.

Explanation for older children

A goal is something you want to achieve. It may be big; it may be small. Goal setting is planning the steps in between, and working out how to get there. Think of something you want to do. It could be learning to ride a skateboard, keeping your room tidy, being a better listener. Anything you want to do can be set as a goal. A goal can be something right now, a week from now or a year from now. Some goals can be many years from now, like travelling the world or changing the world! Goals are easier to keep track of when they are written down, realistic and broken down into smaller steps.

Explanation for younger children

Anything you want to do, like learn to ride a bike without trainer wheels, swim from one end of the pool to the other, or ride a skateboard down a hill, is called a 'goal'. A goal is a kind of wish or dream you would like to come true. To get to your goal you have to plan some steps along the way. You have to take action! If your goal were to ride a bike without trainer wheels, you would make a plan about taking one trainer wheel off at a time, first one, then the other, and practise lots! Eventually, with enough time and practice you will reach your goal.

A young person who set and reached their goals:

Brittany Bergquist: Cell Phones for Soldiers

When Brittany Bergquist was just 13 years old, she and her younger brother, Robbie, heard about a soldier returning from Iraq with a phone bill of almost $8,000 from calling his family at home. Brittany and Robbie wondered why soldiers who sacrifice so much for others couldn't call home for free. Together they set a **GOAL**. They wanted to pay off as much as they could of the soldier's bill. It started with $21 from their piggy banks, followed by lots of lunch money and holding car washes. They got such a buzz after reaching their

GOAL that they decided to keep going. Surely, more soldiers could do with their support. That's when 'Cell Phones for Soldiers' was born.

To reach their **GOAL** they came up with a plan to recycle used cell (mobile) phones. With the money they raised through this and other donations, they purchased prepaid international phone cards for troops around the world. Since 2004, they have sent 181 million minutes of talk time overseas and recycled more than 10.8 million phones. Nothing is going to stop Brittany and Robbie, who have just started 'Helping Heroes Home' which is all about supporting war veterans to reconnect with family life and beyond after war.

For more information on Cell Phones for Soldiers visit www.cellphones forsoldiers.com

GROUP DISCUSSION AND BRAINSTORM

The central concept is 'goals'. Offer your students the following questions:

What is a goal?
What was Brittany and Robbie's goal?
What might have motivated them to set a goal for themselves that benefited other people instead of themselves?
What might help people reach goals?
What might get in the way of people reaching goals?
Can goals connect with each other?
What motivates people to set goals and work towards them?

Finding strengths

When you know and understand your strengths you have a strong platform for self-confidence. Many children, particularly those with learning and behavioural difficulties, can feel discouraged when their hard work doesn't pay off because of their learning and social emotional challenges. The focus turns to their difficulties instead of their strengths. This negative bias lowers resilience and sense of wellbeing. While constructive criticism and realistic feedback are always important, returning the focus to strengths and abilities provides young people with extra stamina and confidence. It can be very useful to encourage young people to use one of their strengths in a new way each day to build their wellbeing (Gander et al., 2012).

BRAINSTORM: Strengths

The central concept is 'strengths'.

What is a personal strength?
Does everyone have strengths?
How are strengths useful?
Can you lose a strength?
Can you build a weakness into a strength?
What is the difference between mental and physical strength?
What are some examples of strengths?

The subconscious mind in goal setting

A short conversation for younger and older students . . .

The 'subconscious' part of your mind helps you more than you could ever imagine. Your subconscious is responsible for 90 per cent (that's almost ALL) of the decisions you make every day. The subconscious mind is super-polite – it never ignores you! It believes everything you say.

Your subconscious mind is important for reaching your goals. When you set a goal it imagines it right there as if it's already been reached. (It doesn't even know you haven't reached that goal yet!) If you imagine yourself taking steps and reaching your goals, your subconscious mind builds the connections in your brain you need to make it happen. Your subconscious never ignores you, so if you tell yourself you can't do something or that you'll never reach that goal, it believes you and imagines just that. Don't get too excited though – if you imagine you will have superpowers to control all the grown-ups in the world, it won't happen, because your goal isn't realistic.

Researchers have found that imagining good things happening, like reaching your goals, has an added bonus. It increases your wellbeing and makes you feel happier (Koo et al., 2008).

Subconscious wellbeing visualisation

Visualisations are a great way to reinforce the subconscious for all of your students' goals. Give them some practice with the process by offering the following visualisation.

You are walking alone through a beautiful lush green valley. You can smell the flowers all around tempting you to pick them. In the distance the wind whispers through the beautiful big trees framing the valley. The warmth of the sun embraces your back and you enjoy its comfort. You are happy to be alive. Your body feels strong. Your skin and bones feel nourished. Your mind is at peace. You feel grateful to be in such a beautiful place and you begin to think about the people you like and love. You start with the ones who make you smile and laugh. You breathe joyfully as you remember a funny time together. You like them a lot and you know they like you too. Next you think about your family. The people you love. You imagine them walking beside you and you feel the strength of their love for you. You feel stronger and wiser when they are near. You are grateful. You stretch your body up fully as if you are trying to reach the big blue sky above. You feel your body tingling with strength and energy. You feel good. As you look ahead you see a big basket of fresh fruit. Your eyes sparkle as you pick up the juiciest fruit you have ever seen. You take a bite and enjoy its sweet flavours. Your body tingles as you take another bite. You quietly tell yourself, 'I am full of health and energy. I feel happy to be alive.'

Goal setting subconscious visualisation

Goal: to ride without training wheels

Subconscious visualisation: you see your bike sparkling in the rich warm sunlight as you walk towards it at the bike track. The birds are chirping all around. You stretch your arms up high. Your body is strong and balanced. The sun is glowing and warming you. Your favourite smell sizzles in the background as your family prepare a barbecue for dinner. You are ready for the challenge. You take hold of your bike and feel proud that it's yours. The trainer wheels are off. You climb on and take a deep, slow breath. Your body is full of energy. The power in your legs is buzzing with excitement and fear. You find all the courage in your heart and you push off. You're moving! Bang, you're down! Ouch! You get up again. You breathe slowly and deeply. You encourage yourself and say quietly, 'I can do this.' You're off again. This time you make it a little further. It's fun! Bang! You're down again. You remember your body is strong and balanced. In a few moments you can celebrate your hard work with a delicious hot sausage. You will not give up. You smile. You feel confident. You feel full of courage. You're off. You're fast! You're surprised! The wind flies through your hair and you enjoy the breeze it brings you. The smile on your face is bigger than you can believe. This is the best fun ever! You are doing it! You're really doing it!!!!

Creating a personal goal setting visualisation

Students can write their own visualisation where they reach a long-term goal – one that might be weeks, months or even years away. Allow them time to write about the steps that will take them there. Remind them to add all five senses to their visualisation. The most effective visualisations incorporate what you see, hear, smell, touch and taste along the way.

You can help your students create something visual by suggesting it is something that looks like a road map with bends and turns, complete with directions along the way. Remind them to keep this in a place they can easily see and to imagine themselves travelling along that road and reaching their goal. Younger students can draw their goals in their visualisation. The challenge is to engage the senses in the drawing!

Strengths identification

Older students (upper primary onwards) can take a character strengths survey online at www.viacharacter.org. For younger students, try making up your own cards showing strengths based on the class brainstorm, or on the character strengths identified at www.viacharacter.org

Strong hands (strengths summary)

Hand out some construction paper and let students trace around their hands. Each finger will represent a strength. For students who have completed the strengths survey at www.viacharacter.org, each finger can represent one of their top five signature strengths. For younger students the hand could be enlarged on A3 card to leave plenty of room for drawings. Help young students work out the five most meaningful strengths to them. Students who can't read or write can draw pictures instead, with an adult writing the strength for them.

Once everyone has written their key strengths on their hand, cut and paste them onto a poster, 'Our class/group lives, works and plays from our strengths.' When anyone in the class/group is struggling, they have a quick reference point to see what strengths they can use to get through the challenge. Students can also have their own strength poster displaying all of the strengths they identified in the activity.

Some classrooms have created bar graphs as an extension of this activity to see where the class strengths are strongest and still developing.

Goal shooting

Take students outdoors or into a gym. Have plenty of basketballs ready for the challenge and enthusiastically show them how to shoot a hoop. (Don't worry if your technique is a bit off – students love to see adults goof around and struggle! If your skill leaves a lot to be desired it provides a great opportunity to show persistence, determination and humility.) Ask if anyone knows where the strongest muscles in our bodies are (they are in your bottom and legs). Pushing from a squat position using the strength of your bottom and leg muscles, aim a ball towards the hoop. Next, shoot for the hoop without squatting using only the strength from your arms. Ask your students which aim looked stronger and more accurate.

Allow some time playing basketball or taking turns shooting hoops, then sit together in a group. Ask, 'Can anyone think how shooting goals using your strongest muscles can teach us something about reaching goals?'

7 steps to my goal: guide sheet and worksheet

Hand out the '7 steps to my goals' guide sheet and worksheet found at the end of this chapter. Allow some time to discuss the guide sheet and help students set a realistic short-term goal.

Goal stories

Prepare to tell your students about a goal you have achieved and a goal you have not yet achieved. If you prefer not to disclose something personal tell the story below as if it was your own:

I want to tell you a story about someone I know. Ever since he started school he was excited about learning to read. Learning to read turned out to be the hardest thing he ever did. You see, he had dyslexia. That meant the letters and words kind of had a mind of their own and didn't appear in order for him as they do for most of you. There wasn't a day where he didn't want to give up. Reading was hard, harder than he ever imagined. The only thing that kept him going was a picture on his wall of Michael Jordan saying, 'the only losers are those who never tried'. So he kept going in each day with the goal to learn to read. He got help, lots of help. He worked out that his strengths were persistence and kindness. He used persistence to keep going and kindness to offer help back to the people helping him. Eventually reading became easier. It was never easy, but it became easier. I remember him telling me when he finished school that he felt ALIVE, RELIEVED and even SURPRISED after reaching his goal. He felt every excruciating moment of effort and persistence was worth it and he knew he had a good future of learning and working ahead of him.

Goal talk (encouraging yourself)

A short conversation with your students . . .

Ask your students, would they encourage a friend working towards a goal or tell them to give up? Sometimes we can be nicer to our friends than we are to ourselves! It is clearly a much better idea to encourage ourselves to reach a goal than to tell ourselves it's impossible. Make mention here that it is important to choose goals carefully and aim for ones that are realistic. Once those goals are chosen, talking to yourself in an encouraging and constructive way energises your brain and it becomes more optimistic!

Worksheet: 'Can I? – Can't I?' achieve my goals?

Hand out the 'Can I? – Can't I?' worksheet found at the end of the chapter. This worksheet allows students to look at the different ways people speak to themselves while working towards a goal.

Younger students can learn from this activity as a quiz. If they think the goal talk is encouraging and constructive they can clap their hands. If the goal talk is not encouraging or constructive they can shake their heads in disapproval.

HOW TO

Role plays: goal setting

Offer the following goal setting problems to your students and ask them to solve them through role plays together. The role plays are all about obstacles that get in the way of reaching a goal. Remind students to include the following in each solution:

ROLE PLAY

1   A plan to reach the goal despite the obstacle.
2   At least one self-encouraging statement to feed the subconscious.
3   Steps to reach the goal.

The goal setting guide sheet at the end of the chapter may be a helpful prompt here.

You plan to audition for the lead in a school play. You have been practising for the part all week. Your best friend has just told you they are going for the same part and asked you to let them go for the part while you go for something else. You really want this part and you know what your friend is asking is not fair. You don't want to lose their friendship but you do want to try out for the part.

You have practised hard for the team try-outs in soccer that are scheduled for tomorrow. While you are walking to school, you trip over. Your ankle aches and you're pretty sure it is sprained.

You want to be team captain for Sports Day. You need a speech prepared. Your teacher tells you the speeches will take place after break time. You got the day mixed up and thought you had a week to prepare. You have no speech prepared but you still want to try for team captain.

You have a maths test in two days and if you get a good mark on the test you earn a dinner out with your family to reward your hard work. You have practised hard and you are looking forward to taking the test. You suddenly fall sick with the flu and will miss the test. What can you do to reach your goal?

You have entered a science competition with two of your best friends. You are making a model together and everything is going well until you end up in a big argument. One of your friends says they quit the project. It is due next week and you have only half of it finished.

You want to learn to roller skate. You arrive at your first roller skating class and the teacher, who is trying to be friendly, teases you about how you keep falling. Everyone looks at you. You are naturally very shy and you find it hard when people put the attention on you – especially when it is embarrassing. You want to find the courage to learn to roller skate.

You have been saving to buy new fish for your aquarium. You have almost raised enough money through extra jobs around the house when you break your dad's coffee machine. He does not look happy. Usually the consequence for breaking things in your house is that you have to replace them using your pocket money.

Goal buddy

Ask students to think of someone they know and trust who is a great example for their particular goal. For a student wanting to increase their fitness it might be a teacher who they have noticed eats healthily and keeps active. Suggest the student talk to this person and let them know they are working towards a goal and that they then ask if the person would be happy to mentor them. Mentoring doesn't have to be complicated – it can be as simple as knowing that someone else who has reached your goal knows about your goal – that in itself can provide great motivation to stay focused. Students can hand out the note below to formalise the buddying experience.

Dear _____,

I am working on _____. I think you are a great example to me of someone who has reached a goal I have set for myself. Would you keep an eye out for me and hand me some tips if you have any? If I am stuck could I ask you for help?

Thank you sincerely, from _____

Self-report school report

Provide students with a blank school report. This is their opportunity to write a report for them to predict how they will do during that term or year. At the end of each term, or the year, they can compare what they wrote with what their teacher(s) wrote. Younger students can write or draw a report for the term rather than year.

Remind students to aim high, be realistic, remember their strengths, be honest and go for it!

Allow students to look at this 'report' mid-term as a reminder of their goals. It can also be looked at when a student is struggling in a particular area. Further extension of this activity can be offered by addressing each subject using the '7 steps to my goal' worksheet.

Step out of your comfort zone

A short conversation with your students . . .

Everyone has a comfort zone. A place where you feel safe and don't feel challenged. A place where you don't have to think or question too hard. When you stay too long in your comfort zone you can find yourself caught up in your own life and experiences without thinking very much about the people around you and what they might be going through. You can also place limits on yourself and what you are capable of doing. Finding the courage to step out of your comfort zone can be an important step towards reaching your full potential. Many things that make you happy also challenge you. When you step out of your comfort zone, there will be healthy risks, mistakes, learning from mistakes, uncertainty, embarrassment and difficulty. Humans are wired to be able to handle all of these things as well as learn and grow from them!

Step out of your comfort zone: discussion in pairs

Think of something you've always wanted to do but haven't done yet. What is it? What excites you about it? Why haven't you done it yet? Do you worry what other people might think about it? What would it take for you to give it a go?

Fast forward – where will I be?

Divide the group into pairs and ask them to imagine they are at a school reunion. For younger students the reunion might be one or two years from now, and for older students it might be ten years. Role play questions similar to the ones below and ask students to try out an interview with their partner. Ask students to try to give answers that reflect their goals. Allow a handful of students to present their interviews to the class if time permits.

Sample interview questions

'Hey, great to see you! How are you?'

'Are you working?' (for younger children this can refer to chores for pocket money)

'Where do you work? What do you do?'

'Are you still playing sport?'

'Do you live alone?'

'Do you go on vacation much?'

'Who are you still friends with from school?

'Were you happy with how you did at school?'

'What are you up to in your spare time?'

'Do you have any hobbies?'

Weekly challenge to further develop the skill

This week's challenge is to set yourself a challenging goal. Step out of your comfort zone but stay tuned to your instincts. Don't choose a goal that is not safe or sensible! An example might be a person who struggles with learning times tables who sets a goal to learn two sets in one week. They put a plan together, enlist help, come up with positive statements to push them through the challenge, and use their strengths. Or you might be someone who finds public speaking really stressful. Your goal might be to stand up at school assembly and present something about your class.

Parent tips

Expect the best for your child

Always maintain high (but realistic) standards for your children's behaviour, attitude and overall achievement. Provide clear boundaries about what you will and won't accept from them, and congratulate them on their efforts to reach goals. Show your child you have faith in them reaching realistic goals – especially those that are important to them and utilise their strengths.

Allow your child to be responsible for their goals – avoid rescuing them

It can be challenging for any parent to watch their child set goals, then lose motivation and get distracted with something else. This is particularly difficult when you see your child miss out on one opportunity after another because they gave up on their goals. Instead of reminding them excessively or, worse, completing steps towards their goals for them, try sitting down with them and trying to work out what is not working for them in goal setting. Is the goal too far away? Has the goal not been broken down into small enough steps? Has something been overlooked? Is your child even motivated to achieve the goal? Look over the areas offered in this chapter for additional inspiration about what helps keep students focused and motivated by their goals. Encourage your child to persist and show your confidence, but, ultimately, this is their learning opportunity – whether that will be through achievement or failure.

Empathise

Let your child know you understand how tough it is to work towards a goal. Listen actively and generously. Try not to problem solve for them, but show them you understand their feelings and frustrations.

Share your goal achievements and failures

Openly discuss your strengths and difficulties when it comes to reaching for a goal. Let them know what works for you and what holds you back. Your child is most likely to listen to these stories when you share them incidentally as they occur or when you tell them in a fun way rather than in a way that sounds a little like a lecture! When you don't reach a goal, tell them about it. Talk about your feelings and let them know what you plan to do about it and what you learnt from your mistakes.

Role model goal setting

Regularly set physical, mental and learning goals for yourself. Write them down where your children can see them. Talk about them at family meals and ask your children to encourage you to reach them.

Encourage

When your child says they will never reach their goal or talks unkindly about themselves and their abilities, encourage them without praising or reassuring them. Simply say something like, 'I can see it's hard to see the end of this. You have worked hard and everyone needs a break. You will get there. How about we take a day off and enjoy a rest', or, 'This isn't meant to be easy. I am proud of how far you've come and I am really enjoying watching you nail every step along the way. You're close!'

You can also tell them you will not allow them to talk about someone they love in that way! You can tell them, 'Don't be mean to yourself. I won't have anyone speak about you like that – including you!'

Create family goals

Sit down together as a family at least a couple of times a year and talk together about what your goals as a family are. Is it to have more fun? Be more organised? More active? To learn new skills together? Write these goals down, breaking them down into many steps. Display them, and revisit them as often as you like as you work towards them together.

Encourage age-appropriate independence

While it can be tempting to do everything for your children, either to save time or to keep the peace, the more you do for them the less capable they feel. Feeling capable is essential for resilience. When you feel capable you know you can handle life's challenges, whether it is getting yourself a snack when you're hungry, or being able to walk home from school on your own. Confidence comes from engaging in many things that make you feel capable. Helping around the house, garden and neighbourhood develops important skills for life. While many young people express their desire not to help out, most feel a great sense of accomplishment once they have helped. If helping becomes a non-negotiable part of family life, over time children get used to 'just doing it'! The complaining part is sometimes to be expected, but persist through as much as you can. The pay-off is someone with more skills and a greater sense of independence who feels proud of their contribution. Always consider age and safety when increasing independence and show your child you have confidence in them to rise to the challenge.

7 STEPS TO MY GOAL

1. **My goal is:**

2. **Which area of my life my goal belongs in:**

(Sport/friendships/learning/health/fitness/family)

3. **How I can reach my goal:**

(The steps I can take to get there)

4. **My strengths:**

(Things I'm good at that will help me reach my goal)

5. **When?**

(How soon I would like to reach my goal)

6. **Who are the people who can help me reach my goal?**

7. **Check? Did I work towards my goal today?**

M	T	W	Th	F	Sa	Su
☐	☐	☐	☐	☐	☐	☐
☐	☐	☐	☐	☐	☐	☐
☐	☐	☐	☐	☐	☐	☐

Celebrate if I've worked towards my goal for 7 days!

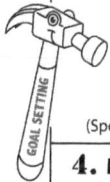

GOAL SETTING

7 STEPS TO MY GOAL

1. My goal is:

2. Which area of my life my goal belongs in: (sport/friendships/learning/health/fitness/family)

3. How I can reach my goal: (the steps I can take to get there)

4. My strengths: (things I'm good at that will help me reach my goal)

PERSISTENCE

5. When? (how soon I would like to reach my goal)

6. Who are the people who can help me reach my goal?

7. Check? Did I work towards my goal today?

Mon ☐	Tues ☐	Wed ☐	Thur ☐	Fri ☐	Sat ☐	Sun ☐
Mon ☐	Tues ☐	Wed ☐	Thur ☐	Fri ☐	Sat ☐	Sun ☐
Mon ☐	Tues ☐	Wed ☐	Thur ☐	Fri ☐	Sat ☐	Sun ☐

Celebrate if I've worked towards my goal for 7 days!

7 STEPS TO MY GOAL

This guide sheet helps remind students of the steps which help get you closer to reaching your goals.

1. My goal is:

To move from B grade soccer to A grade soccer

2. Which area of my life my goal belongs in: (sport/friendships/learning/health/fitness/family)

SPORT (Soccer)

3. How I can reach my goal: (the steps I can take to get there) Talk to my coach.
Ask what's the difference between being chosen for B grade and A grade. Find out what skills I need to build on. Write practice times on my homework timetable

4. My strengths: (things I'm good at that will help me reach my goal)

Persistent, hard worker, energetic, competitive

5. When? (how soon I would like to reach my goal)

Make the A grade by next season in one year.

6. Who are the people who can help me reach my goal? Ask mum and dad to help by practising with me on weekends. Ask my coach to give me honest feedback on where I need to work harder. I will help myself by encouraging myself.

7. Check? Did I work towards my goal today?

Mon	☑	Tues	☑	Wed	☐	Thur	☑	Fri	☑	Sat	☑	Sun	☐
Mon	☐	Tues	☑	Wed	☑	Thur	☑	Fri	☑	Sat	☐	Sun	☑
Mon	☑	Tues	☑	Wed	☑	Thur	☑	Fri	☑	Sat	☑	Sun	☑

Celebrate if I've worked towards my goal for 7 days!

GOAL SETTING

PERSISTENCE

KEEPING CALM

'CAN I? - CAN'T I?'

Circle the 'self talk' that is **encouraging** and **helpful** and gives your brain the message, 'I can do it.'

Note to facilitator: Younger students can do this as a quiz read aloud to them. If they think the 'self talk' is **encouraging** and **helpful** they clap their hands. If they think it is discouraging and **unhelpful** they shake their heads.

Circle the encouraging and helpful 'self talk'.

I am practising every day and it will pay off · Practising is a waste of time. I'm no good at this

This is tough and I am tougher · This is tough, I can't handle this

I'm so tired! I can't do this anymore · I am tired and I am not giving up

I am going to make it · I'm not going to make it

No one cares, no one will help · Someone will help

The hard work is worth it - I will get there · I'm wasting my time and I'm not getting anywhere

This is taking too long · Anything worthwhile usually takes time and practice

Write an **encouraging** and **helpful** 'self talk' statement to fix the ones below. Younger students can brainstorm the answers.

1. I hate language lessons. Who needs to learn a language anyway? _____

_____

2. No one likes me _____

_____

_____

3. I will never be able to learn this, it's too hard _____

_____

_____

_____

Reference list

Gander, F. et al. 2012. 'Strength-Based Positive Interventions: Further Evidence for Their Potential in Enhancing Well-Being'. *Journal of Happiness Studies* Vol. 14, pp. 1241–1259.

Koo, M. et al. 2008. 'It's a Wonderful Life: Mentally Subtracting Positive Events Improves People's Affective States, Contrary to Their Affective Forecasts'. *Journal of Personality and Social Psychology* Vol. 95 No. 5, pp. 1217–1224.

Mehta, M. 2013. *The Entrepreneurial Instinct: How Everyone Has the Innate Ability to Start a Successful Business*. New York: McGraw-Hill.

Schunk, D. H. 1991. 'Self-Efficacy and Academic Motivation'. *Educational Psychologist* Vol. 26, pp. 207–231.

Schunk, D. H. and Zimmerman, B. 2006. *Motivation and Self-Regulated Learning: Theory Research and Application*. London: Taylor & Francis.

Recommended reading for young people

Amnesty International. 2008. *We Are All Born Free: The Universal Declaration of Human Rights in Pictures*. London: Frances Lincoln Children's Books.

Carlson, N. 1994. *How to Lose All Your Friends*. Melbourne: Viking Press.

Carlson, R. 2000. *Don't Sweat the Small Stuff for Teens: Simple Ways to Keep Your Cool in Stressful Times*. New York: Random House.

Christ, J. 2006. *What to Do When You're Sad and Lonely: A Guide for Kids*. Minneapolis, MN: Free Spirit Publishing.

Cook, J. 2011. *I Just Don't Like the Sound of No*. Boys Town, NE: Boys Town Press.

Covey, S. 2008. *The 7 Habits of Happy Kids* and *The 7 Habits of Highly Effective Teens*. New York: Simon and Schuster.

Greenspon, T. 2007. *What to Do When Good Enough Isn't Good Enough: The Real Deal on Perfectionism*. Minneapolis, MN: Free Spirit Publishing.

Huebner, D. 2008. *What to Do When Your Temper Flares*; *What to Do When You Worry Too Much*; *What to Do When Your Habits Take Hold*. Washington, DC: Magination Books.

Johnston, N. 2008. *Go Away Mr Worry Thoughts*. Melbourne: Nicky's Art Publishing.

McCloud, C. 2011. *Growing Up with a Bucket Full of Happiness: Three Rules to a Happier Life*. Brighton, MI: Bucket Fillers Inc.

McIntyre, T. 2013. *The Survival Guide for Kids with Behaviour Challenges: How to Make Good Choices and Stay Out of Trouble*. Minneapolis, MN: Free Spirit Publishing.

Moroney, T. 2008. *When I'm Feeling Lonely*; *When I'm Feeling Sad*; *When I'm Feeling Angry*; *When I'm Feeling Scared*; *When I'm Feeling Happy*; *When I'm Feeling Kind*. Melbourne: The Five Mile Press.

Parr, T. 2003. *The Feel Good Book* and *The Okay Book*. Sydney: ABC Books.

Pett, M. 2011. *The Girl Who Never Made Mistakes*. Naperville, IL: Sourcebooks Jabberwocky Publishing.

Salzburg, B. 2010. *Beautiful Oops*. New York: Workman Publishing Company.

Smout, K. 2015. *When Life Sucks for Kids: Ideas and Tips for When You Feel Mad, Worried or Sad*. Adelaide: Published by author.

Spelman, C. M. 2003. *When I Feel Good About Myself*. Sydney: Scholastic Inc.

Verdick, E. 2004. *Words Are Not for Hurting*. Minneapolis, MN: Free Spirit Publishing.

Whitford, R. and Selway, M. 2007. *Sleepy Little Yoga*. London: Random House.

Useful websites on child development, resilience, stress management and wellbeing

www.kidsmatter.edu.au

www.cyh.com

www.theresilienceproject.com.au

www.whatsthebuzz.net.au

www.wellbeingaustralia.com.au

www.embracethefuture.org.au

www.beyondblue.org.au

www.youthbeyondblue.com

www.headspace.org.au

www.siblingsaustralia.org.au

www.copmi.net.au (children of parents with a mental illness)

www.worrywisekids.org

www.natureplaysa.org.au

www.randomactsofkindness.org

www.theworldkindnessmovement.org

www.cultureofempathy.com

Index

active mood combat (AMC) 27, 38
adrenalin 118–19, 122
amygdala 118–19, 122
anger worksheets 148–9
authenticity 41, 42; parent tips 54–7

balloon push 132–3
balloons in a box 79–80
baseline, measuring outcomes and 12
be my eyes and be my ears 75
be the boss of problem solving
    (BOSS): guide sheet 113; practice
    activities 101–4
brainstorming: feeling left out 69;
    feelings and values 43, 45, 49, 63;
    form 14; goals 194; gratitude 21;
    optimism 21; persistence 172;
    perspective 21; problem solving
    104; strengths 195; stress 121;
    working hard 173
breathing exercises 101, 123–4
bullying: role plays 83–4; between
    siblings 87
butter making 176–7

cake bake-off roster 78–9
calendar of celebrations 53
card towers 177–8
celebrations 12; calendar of 53
chatterboxes 160–1
check-in time 11
class encouragement pigeon holes
    78

clay balls 135
comfort zone, stepping out of 202–3
community and connection 66–94;
    balloons in a box 79–80; be
    my eyes and be my ears 75;
    brainstorming 69; building a
    reputation 72; cake bake-off
    roster 78–9; class encouragement
    pigeon holes 78; community
    building 85–6; community tubs 76;
    connect-a-thon sponsorship 71,
    92; empathy: how will you take
    action? worksheet 70, 91; example
    69; group discussion 69; hold the
    smile 71; individual contributions
    in class 76–8; introduction 66–7;
    kindness record sheet 94; me in
    here 82; me three 82; one world,
    so many ideas! 75; parent tips
    86–90; pass the smile 71; peer
    mentoring 82; practice 70, 75, 76,
    79, 82; role plays 72–4, 83–4;
    sandstone sculptures 80; school
    volunteer network 78; schools,
    role in 67–8; shared memories 81;
    smile, receiving a 70–1; statement
    to build relationships 70; student-
    teacher interviews 80–1; teacher
    reports 81, 93; understanding
    68–9; we can work this out
    together 80; weekly challenge 86;
    well wishing 79; who's looking out
    for me? 75

community gardens 85

community tubs 76

compromise: journal entry 105–6; persistence and 183; problem solving 97, 104–5; reaching agreement on 107

conflict, handling 88–9

connect-a-thon sponsorship 71, 92

Csikszentmihalyi, M. 130, 131

cultural diversity 53, 56, 75

curiosity/judgement quiz 155

curiosity vs. judgement debates 155–6

disappointment, space for 164

'to do' lists 132

dopamine 191

Dweck, C. 9, 170

empathy 68; example 69; how will you take action? worksheet 70, 91; role plays 73–4

encouragement rather than praise 8–9, 180–1

exercise for wellbeing 29

feedback on teachers 81, 93

feelings on the spot 133

'fight or flight' response 118–19, 122

fingerprints 52, 109

'flow' 130; and embracing challenge 130–1; encouraging 139; survey 146

friendships: curiosity in 159–60; curiosity in, challenge 160; outside school 86, 89

geocaching 165

goal buddies 201–2

goals, setting 191–210; brainstorming 194, 195; can I? – can't I? worksheet 200, 210; example 193–4; and finding strengths 194–5; goal buddy 201–2; goal shooting 198; goal talk 199; group discussion 194; introduction 191–3; motivating students in 192–3; parent tips 204–6; practice 197; problem solving 102–3; role plays 200–1; self-report school report 202; stepping out of comfort zone 202–3; steps to my goal guide and worksheet 198, 207–9; stories 199; strengths identification 197; strengths survey 197; strong hands (strength summary) 197–8; subconscious goal setting visualisation 196–7; subconscious mind in 195; subconscious wellbeing visualisation 196; understanding 193; weekly challenge 204; where will I be? 203–4

Goodman, R. N. 12

gratitude: 7 day record sheet 28, 39; 21 day check-in 28; brainstorming 21; to emergency services 29; example 20; hot and cold 28; introduction 18–19; journals 27, 28, 35–6; parent tips 33–6; photo/illustration board 28; practice 27, 28, 29, 32; role plays 29; sticky notes 29; understanding 19–20; wants versus needs run 30

grit and persistence 170

growth mindset and persistence 170

guided meditation 128–9
gut feelings 43–4

helpful thinking *see* optimism (helpful thinking/high side)
high side *see* optimism (helpful thinking/high side)
high side and low side relay 31–2
high side walk 32
hobbies 159; challenge 159
hot and cold 28
human chain 178

ice cube challenge 176
independence, age-appropriate 206
integrity: brainstorming 49; example 42–3; group discussion on honesty and 46, 50; oath 46–7; repairing lost 47–8; respect and reputation 49–50; role plays 47–8, 48–9

jigsaw puzzle 179
jokes 132
journals 10–11; blank page 15; compromise entry 105–6; curiosity 157; friendships outside school 86; gratitude 27, 28, 35–6; reflective thinking activity 45–6; self-reflection activity 46–7

Kauai longitudinal study 66
keeping calm 118–50; anger worksheets 148–9; balloon push 132–3; body reactions to stress 118–19, 122; brainstorming 121; breathing exercises 123–4; calming ideas worksheet 123, 126, 143; class stress bar graph 121; clay balls 135; 'to do' lists 132; early warning signs worksheet 122, 142; embracing challenge 130–1; example 120–1; feelings on the spot 133; 'flow' 130, 139; 'flow' survey 146; group discussion 121; guided meditation 128–9; how big does this rate? worksheet 124, 145; introduction 118–19; jokes 132; mindfulness 124–5, 138; parent tips 136–41; playlist 131; positive visualisation exercise 126; positive words jar 132; practice 123, 124, 125, 126, 128, 130, 131, 133, 135, 136; progressive muscle relaxation 133–4; recipe invention 131; role plays 126–8; silence is bliss 135, 139; silent bird count 135; stress less goal setting challenge 123; stress less plan 123, 144; tricks to keep calm 147; understanding stress 119–20; weekly challenge 136
kindness record sheet 94
knots 178

laughter 132
learning difficulties 185
lies 52–3; role plays 48–9
listening well 89
local councils 85; surveys 90
low side *see* pessimism (unhelpful thinking/low side)

massage 140
material possessions 34
me in here 82
me three 82

measuring a baseline and outcomes 12
meditation, guided 128–9
mental resilience activities 108
mentoring 201–2; peer 82
mindfulness 124–5, 138
mirror neurons 68
mistakes and curiosity 151–68; 'best mistake ever' worksheet 156, 166; chatterboxes 160–1; curiosity in friendships 159–60; curiosity in friendships challenge 160; curiosity/judgement quiz 155; curiosity vs. judgement debates 155–6; example 153; group discussion and brainstorming 154; hobbies 159; hobby challenge 159; introduction 151–2; journal activity 157; mistake of the day 156–7; parent tips 137, 163–5; practice 155, 156, 157, 158; questions to encourage self-awareness 167; role plays 157–9; rubber bands 161; scientific experiments 162; understanding 152; weekly challenge 162; what's in the box? 161–2
mobile devices 88
moods 7–8; active mood combat (AMC) 27, 38; low side and 26; mood check-in 27
motivation: and persistence 170–1, 173–4; survey 174, 188
muscle relaxation, progressive 133–4
music, class 131

nature: indoors 141; play 140
negative bias 19, 21

neighbourhood: play 89; walks 85
neuroplasticity 8
nursing homes 85–6

oaths, integrity 46–7
observation activity 101–2
one more minute! 176
one world, so many ideas! 75
optimism (helpful thinking/high side): bake off 33; brainstorming 21; high side/low side guide sheet 22, 37; high side/low side relay 31–2; high side walk 32; parent tips 35, 36; and pessimism 18–19, 20; role plays 22–6; showing 36; understanding 19–20; weekly challenge 33
The Optimistic Child 96
origami 179

paper clip/pipe cleaner sculptures 177
parents, tips for: community and connection 86–90; gratitude, perspective and optimism 33–6; keeping calm 136–41; mistakes and curiosity 163–5; persistence 180–5; problem solving 110–12; setting goals 204–6; values 54–7
peer: mentoring 82; relationships 12
persistence 168–90; brainstorming 172, 173; buttery bliss 176–7; card towers 177–8; challenge worksheet 173, 187; example 172; grit and 170; group discussion 172; growth mindset and 170; human chain 178; ice cube challenge 176; introduction 169–71; jigsaw puzzle 179; knots

178; motivation and 170–1, 173–4;
motivation survey 174, 188;
mountains of, guide sheet 173,
186; one more minute! 176;
origami 179; paper clip/pipe
cleaner sculptures 177; parent
tips 180–5; practice 173, 176,
179; role plays 174–5; rubber
band cork/block challenge
178–9; understanding 171;
weekly challenge 179–80
perspective: brainstorming 21;
developing 19; how big does
this rate? worksheet 124, 145;
maintaining a balanced 33;
parent tips 33
pessimism (unhelpful thinking/low
side): high side/low side guide
sheet 22, 37; high side/low side
relay 31–2; and moods 26; and
optimism 18–19, 20; role plays
22–6; understanding 19–20
photo/illustration board 28
playlist, class 131
plus and minus solutions 98, 114
positive visualisation exercise 126
positive words jar 132
praise, encouragement rather than
8–9, 180–1
problem solving 96–117; BOSS
activities 101–4; BOSS guide
sheet 113; brainstorming 104;
breathing techniques 101;
compromise 104–7; example 98;
fingerprints 109; goal setting
activity 102–3; introduction 96–7;
journal activity 105–6; mental
resilience activities 108;
observation activity 101–2;

parent tips 110–12; plus and
minus solutions worksheet 98,
114; practice 101–4, 105, 107,
109; puzzle me 109; riddles 107,
116; role plays 99–100, 102–3;
seeking solution activity 103–4;
through disagreement 107,
115; treasure hunt 107–8;
understanding 97; weekly
challenge 109; work with one
hand 108
program values 3
progressive muscle relaxation
133–4
puzzle me 109

recipe invention 131
reflective thinking journal activity
45–6
relationships: classroom 12; family
86–7
reminders, learning through repetition
and 11
reputation: building a good 72;
respect and integrity 49–50; role
plays 72–3
respectful behaviour 54–5
responsibilities and roles in
classroom 76–8
riddles 107, 116
role plays: bullying 83–4; empathy
73–4; gratitude 29; high and low
side 22–6; keeping calm 126–8;
learning from mistakes 157–9;
persistence 174–5; problem
solving 99–100, 102–3; repairing
lost integrity 47–8; reputation
72–3; setting goals 200–1; truth
and lies 48–9

roles and responsibilities in
   classroom 76–8
rubber band cork/block challenge
   178–9
rubber bands 161

sandstone sculptures 80
school report, self-report 202
school volunteer network 78
schools, building community and
   connection 67–8
scientific experiments 162
self-assessment: effort 189; self-
   rating scale 16; and self-reflection
   9–10; survey 12; teaching your
   child 182
self-awareness, questions to
   encourage 167
self-esteem 8–9
self-reflection: journal activity 46–7;
   and self-assessment 9–10
self-report school report 202
Seligman, M. 18, 19, 51, 66, 96
sessions: adjusting pace and content
   6–8; duration 6; structure 3–6
silence: is bliss 135; practising 139
silent bird count 135
singing 35, 140
smile: hold the 71; pass the 71;
   receiving a 70–1
smiling mind APP 125
Social Emotional Learning (SEL)
   programs 13
social media 56
sponsorship, connect-a-thon 71, 92
sticky notes, gratitude 29
strengths: brainstorming 195; finding
   194–5; summary 197–8; survey
   197

Strengths and Difficulties
   Questionnaire 12
stress: body reactions to 118–19,
   122; brainstorming 121; class bar
   graph 121; early warning signs
   worksheet 122, 142; group
   discussion 121; less goal setting
   challenge 123; less plan 123, 144;
   understanding 119–20; *see also*
   keeping calm
student and teacher: interviews
   80–1; relationships 12; shared
   memory 81
subconscious: goal setting
   visualisation 196–7; wellbeing
   visualisation 196
surveys: going with the 'flow' 146;
   local councils 90; motivation
   174, 188; self-assessment 12;
   strengths 197; 'Things bigger than
   me' 50–1, 64

teacher and student: interviews
   80–1; relationships 12; shared
   memory 81
teacher reports 81, 93
thank you notes 34–5
'things bigger than me' survey 50–1,
   64
treasure hunt 107–8
truth and lies role play 48–9

unhelpful thinking *see* pessimism
   (unhelpful thinking/low side)

values 41–65; brainstorming 43, 45,
   49, 63; and cultural diversity 53,
   56; differences in 45; example
   42–3; family 54–7; finding my

values guide and worksheet 44, 58, 59; fingerprints 52; group discussion 46, 50; gut feelings 43–4; if it was up to me worksheet 50, 63; if no one was watching 48; integrity, respect and reputation 49–50; introduction 41; me and my favourite things worksheet 44, 61; for my resilience and wellbeing guide sheet 46, 62; oaths 46–7; parent tips 54–7; practice 44, 45, 51, 53; project 51–2; reflective thinking journal activity 45–6; repairing lost integrity 47–8; resilience and wellbeing toolbox 3; role plays 47–8, 48–9; self-reflection journal activity 46–7; standing up for, challenge 53–4; 'things bigger than me' survey 50–1, 64; understanding 42; vision statement 51; weekly challenge 53; who am I? worksheet 44, 60

vision statement 51

visualisation: positive 126; subconscious goal setting 196–7; subconscious wellbeing 196

volunteer network 78

wants versus needs run 30

we can work this out together 80

weekly themes 11

well wishing 79

what's in the box? 161–2

who's looking out for me? 75

work with one hand 108

yoga 31, 140